MW01393961

A Much Closer Look
AT THE KING JAMES HOLY BIBLE

Professor Roy Yonce

RoseDog❧Books

PITTSBURGH, PENNSYLVANIA 15222

The contents of this work including, but not limited to, the accuracy of events, people, and places depicted; opinions expressed; permission to use previously published materials included; and any advice given or actions advocated are solely the responsibility of the author, who assumes all liability for said work and indemnifies the publisher against any claims stemming from publication of the work.

All Rights Reserved
Copyright © 2010 by Professor Roy Yonce
No part of this book may be reproduced or transmitted
in any form or by any means, electronic or mechanical,
including photocopying, recording, or by any information
storage and retrieval system without permission in
writing from the author.

ISBN: 978-1-4349-8167-7
eISBN: 978-1-4349-4411-5
Printed in the United States of America

First Printing

For more information or to order additional books, please contact:
RoseDog Books
701 Smithfield Street
Pittsburgh, Pennsylvania 15222
U.S.A.
1-800-834-1803
www.rosedogbookstore.com

An Introduction, before the Table of Contents

I want to believe the contents of the KJ Bible (King James Bible) verses but as a researcher of known factual uncovered information, one must not give into just wishful thinking but rely upon the gathered evidence of on hand materials.

The CONTRADICTIONS within the KJ Bible, the UNGODLY WISDOM, and such QUICK BURNING TEMPERS always displayed when wanting always to KILL its very creations every few days points to a MAN WRITTEN BOOK instead of it being a HOLY DEVINE GUIDANCE. I am sorry to say.

I became a cover to cover reader of the FAITHIST BIBLE about 50 years ago. Its name is OAHSPE. I have fully studied it many times. I see no detected contradictions nor no man made biases within it's over 1,000 pages. I have been a frequent reader of this great book, from cover to cover completely. It has become my most favorite book of all times. I study it often.

Here is its WWW address. I have bought dozens of copies for my friends.
http://robertbayer.tripod.com/oahspequotations/

I have also read the CATHOLIC Bible. I attended a private Catholic all boys' high school. Here below is its WWW address. WWW is the Internet, World Wide Web.
http://www.catholicdoors.com/bible/index.htm

I have also read the MORMON (Joseph Smith's book) Bible several times.

I have lived in Utah for several years, the home state of Mormons. Here below is its WWW address. WWW is the Internet, World Wide Web.
http://en.wikipedia.org/wiki/Joseph_Smith_Translation_of_the_Bible

Copyrighted July 2009 by: RoadRunner Electronics Professor Roy Yonce ISBN 978-1-4349-8167-7

I am a nine time reader of the Authorized King James Bible from cover to cover and have completely studied all of its contents.

Here is its WWW address. WWW is the Internet, World Wide Web.

http://quod.lib.umich.edu/k/kjv/

You can decide for yourself as I take you by the hand and disclose several hundred verses from within the KJ

Bible book. As we disclose many discrepancies together. It looks like all the evidence is gathered from one book that it has man's biases of war, killing, rudeness, meanness, not loving, extremely quick hot burning anger tempers with no value in regards to human life. It just can't be any Devine, great wisdom given book from any God of mine. Thank you, Professor Roy Yonce.

Remember that Human Life expectancy has increased only because Humans have developed better guides and recognition of Death's impending dangers. A Longer Life's expectancy has risen over the years and it continues to do so as we learn its courses. Anti-problem Drugs, Vaccinations, Other injections of shots, better suggestions of minimum daily requirements. Avoiding excessive sun exposures and many others. No God Interventions, Just better serious controls of our daily expected needs. I often have heard a parent say after a very serious accident. "God sure saved that person's life". But they ignored the fact that so many other people died in the same accident. No, I do not believe God was responsible for saving that one life just as he/she wasn't responsible for taking all the others. Just laws of the Universe which no one understands yet. The evidence points that way. It helps to prove more and more that all is pre-destined. Psychics have been able to successfully predict many future events that have come true. Many psychics like our modern day Edgar Cayce, Jean Dixson, Dorothy Spence Laurer, Peter Hurkos, Nastradamous, thousands of others, told daily of future events that would happen and they did. No God Interventions has happened.

I see too many sad, miserable things happen in the world for it to be God's fault. I believe God made the world and it's chemicals that put together all climates (weather included) to cause effects but he does not stay the ruler of daily functions to intervene everybody's DNA or what have you. Even their daily lives. Angels might sometimes on occasions but God does not.

I have personally visited the same grounds, exactly in Japan where our Atomic Bombs dropped on their two large Industrial cities back in the 1940's Nagasaki and Hiroshima. Many thousands died instantly, within a few minutes after being cooked to death. More thousands died after they visited and worked at these places while gathering and accumulating radiation doses for years later. No God Interventions.

If one will carefully look with me at the many hundreds of pages in the KJ Bible, one can see many contradictions, mistakes, and errors that no real God would have permitted. It looks like someone before in Biblical times tried to sway the world into believing of a supreme God which takes care of man but modern sciences has slowly proved otherwise.

There are too many Holocaust type happenings, wars continually, deaths of loved ones, better vaccines, more learned expectancy benefits, for any one serious God to be responsible for. No evidence points to him or her ever intervened. Remember, when certain men or women proclaim that they can talk to God. Where are the none-finished Human Owners Manuals? Where are God's words about the Constellation development stories? Where are the real true facts he/she could have told us about DNA, Medicines, Diseases, or any of Life's struggles? Cancer info? Other dozens of Plagues? The Dinosaur age, more truths about creation, more truths about death and hundreds of others? It hasn't happened yet because any man or woman who proclaims to speak with God, only talks about wars and ways to kill more and also to put the contrast of fear in your mind that the day of revenge is coming always soon. In fact, if you read Paul's words in his letter while being in prison a couple thousand years ago, He says the second coming of Christ was just around the corner then. "It was coming soon". All the preachers say that also. Soon, Soon, Soon. I proclaim they do not know what they are talking about.

We have many, many THINGS WE COULD TALK ABOUT by the thousands that are unexplained. But all these men and women who have made their profession proclaiming that they have talked to God almighty, have not passed onto us any great wisdom of his words to help us humans in any field.

I warn you before reading further, I have laid the chips to fall where they do roll. You will see flat out CONTRADICTIONS that no real God would have ever made if he wrote the KJ Bible. (The King at a certain time destroyed many thousands of religious works of art). He wanted to control all the biblical knowledge to future human generations. Here is the WWW address to many old hidden Scrolls found proving more information for support.

http://en.wikipedia.org/wiki/Dead_Sea_scrolls

We have always had groups of people on earth which jump to conclusions and try to control and influence the outcome. Like the earlier group which believed the world was flat. Also others believed the planets moved a certain way was fact until Galileo the scientist proved otherwise. Or that group that insisted otherwise until Albert Einstein proved his theory. How about that group of sun worshipers theory until recently it was discovered that too much sun rays and radiation definitely causes skin cancers? Yes there are plenty of others. Like the present group that actually thinks that Moses spoke regularly, daily with God. Now if you are still in that group, by constantly being brain washed, don't give up! Continue reading this book so you can be intelligently informed about religious contradictions about the latest clues that are being discovered. Just like I told my thousands of college students, Continue to read and study, otherwise, when you are asked to give your opinion on a subject. Unless you have read, you cannot join in the respected debate and be informative as you should.

How about that long ago groups of persons that taxed peoples' houses according to the amount of windows. So the people built their homes with less taxes by less windows until it was discovered that no sun-shine in to kill bacteria caused serious plagues. No God intervened. It was smart people solving the problem but only after thousands and thousands had died.

How did Moses get away with it for so long? I'll answer that, as I proclaim further on in my book. Religion is

BIG, BIG, BIG business with its high tax free and donation deductions. Anyone benefitting from these will not be going to complain much continually. If no tax incentives were ever present, I guarantee you; This Moses story and CONTRADICTIONS would have been uncovered and reported long, long ago.

A change of possible false belief is accomplished by slowly getting the word "God" removed from many places and documents. Prayers taken out of schools and public places. That is one way and it's already in effect by thousands. I am not a member of that group but I see it all the time. Oh do you see that too? It's going to get much, much, much more controlled before it's over. Are you ready? Read my book to see the evidence that is piling up weekly.

"A MUCH CLOSER LOOK AT THE KING JAMES HOLY BIBLE" By: Professor Roy Yonce.

First of all, Let us make the statement that several printed versions of the Holy Bible does exist.

They are out there being distributed, studied and read for as much understandings and comprehensions as possible for all faiths, races and nationalities over the entire globe.

I can remember only a few years ago that I was invited to a major religious establishment and listening to its leaders say that they promote in their organization the ideas daily that their Holy Bible did not have any inconsistencies and even made all attendees verbally state that their Christian religion documents and books had no CONTRADICTIONS. (Which I found were not true). Many versions have hundreds of changes from the original authorized King James Version.

It took me 40 days steady study and research of the entire KJ Bible.
It took me another 40 days to construct my notes into a book style.
It took me another 40 days to type, proofread and reference all materials
It took me another 40 days to Print, Deliver, and distribute the first copies.

TABLE OF CONTENTS

*Some verses are printed to just help to make coherent build up only for this book.
At least _62_ of the _104_ group of verses printed here have contradictions.*

No words have been changed, nor added, nor deleted. Only printed out and pointed to as referenced comments.

Article content   page

Detailed Findings Info Statement iii
Table of Contents xi
Reply with your own E-Mail .... ii, iv, and 2
Copyright Information .... ii, iv, and 2
A Verse from King James Version stating
    Disciple requirements 4
Verse # 1 of 104. Luke 14:25 thru 26. Notice 4
Numerology Info 8
Professor Roy Yonce's personal prayer for others
    to use 19

Author's Brief outline of Experience 24
The Ten Commandments 26
PERIODS OF 40 DAYS IN THE
    HOLY BIBLE 64
What do we know about Moses? 83
Let us return to the story of Moses. 101
Let us return to the story of Moses. 119
Generations listing from God to Jesus.
    (76 Generations). 136
A BIBLICAL EGYPTIAN SLAVE'S
    KNOWLEDGE 140
MODERN, PC APPLICATION PROGRAM
    CALLED BIBLE CODES 160
Picture taken of Professor Roy Yonce in
    about 2004 171
The last of 104 verses from the K J Bible
    NOTICES 195
Reading and taking notes, suggested plan. 197
I wish there was a God to help, Poem 200
End of book 203

This book contains the detailed findings of several (104) meticulous searches that are from the King James Holy Bible.

No words have been changed, nor added, nor deleted. Only printed out and pointed to as referenced comments, so the readers can see and have a much better, clearer possible understanding of this marvelous designed book that tries to prove there is a controlling and helping God for us Earth Humans. A suggested Reading and Note taking Plan has also been included.

This book's printing and also the King James Version book is recommended reading for every adult who lives on the face of this globe. Both this printing and also the King James Version should be read to children so their detailed comprehension can grow with each analyzation period of study regularly. Also suggested that they take notes. Notes written and while reading is where a large percentage of learning and mind remembrances are done.

The King James Holy Bible is not clearly seen nor understood ever on its very first reading. It takes several studies as understanding power and good comprehension to gather the complete putting together of so many elements from the last parts to even understand the beginning parts. It should be read and studied in a sequential order. (The first eight books of the old Testaments, then the first five books of the New Testament for your individual absorption rate. Maybe more or less the Nine times this reader took. It all depends on your available time to spend again and again. But try to understand the details with your note taking.

Better understandings by any individual are done by reading the K J Bible totally from cover to cover. Then this book in its entire contents sequentially.

Copyrighted July 2009 by: RoadRunner Electronics Professor Roy Yonce ISBN 978-1-4349-8167-7

**His own contact E-Mail address:
ProfYonce@NetIns.Net**

Let me kindly suggest that you consider sending me an E-Mail stating when you have read my complete book. What you think of my printed book to alert and teach many worldwide readers a head start on its findings and opinions. It is toward their own research and better understandings.

Please donate a contribution to help promote this book's distribution too many others. We appreciate your kind help where you can.

Thank you, Professor Roy Yonce.

Please include some pictures of you and your family to help us keep an active list of the printing and distribution list with your positive suggestions.

Thank you again.

After all, Synergy Energy is much better than any individual single input!

Just supposing someone at a religious gathering would ask you if you wanted to become a Disciple of Jesus Christ? You would probably say, "Why Sure, Yes!"

"My Sunday school teacher has suggested that many times. I even try to be one of his followers and a chosen Disciple". You might say.

Well not so fast! Let's see if you would still answer yes so quickly. Especially after you have read exactly what Jesus Christ was supposed to have said while on this Earth about becoming one of his devoted Disciples.

Please READ ON.

This book does not print the complete words and connection to let a complete Bible story be told as an understandable complete story. One must read that story from its start to finish from the KJ Bible. This printed book only prints excerpts to point out the detailed occurrence and statements which should be observed to a reader about its integrity and interpretations, especially CONTRADICTIONS and UNTRUTHS throughout the entire K J Bible. This reader had to try to digest all by reading it completely cover to cover nine times, with plenty of note taking on each.

1- See Luke 14:25 thru 26. Printed from the New Testament. This is a contradiction of what we are taught all our life.

> [25] And there went great multitudes with him: and he turned, and said unto them,
>
> [26] If any man come to me, and **hate not** his father, and mother, and wife, and children, and brethren, and sisters, yea, and his own life also, he cannot be my disciple.

When one reads the above verse stating the prerequisites for becoming a disciple for Jesus Christ. We see in clear words that he wanted only a mean, Mixed up person, a "Son-of-a-Bitch" to become his disciple. I can still set a good example without becoming one of his disciples. I do not hate anyone. I definitely do not hate my parents, nor my wife, nor any brothers or sisters, nor myself. That does not say any good about the character of his chosen disciples.

I will never become one of his Disciples because I love and want to help all my children, grandchildren, parents, my wife and no, I do not hate myself. So there you are. I'll bet you are very surprised that he said that. Well, we have many more than just that which was said by him and God in the Old Testament.

I'll bet the many long years, you have attended Sunday school and so many church services, that absolutely no teacher, nor preacher has ever layed that particular verse before you. Otherwise, they may not see you on the following Sunday for your devoted money to help them further.

This is one particular verse where reference meaning elsewhere states that the true meaning is hid from those not educated. The place and how the one word "Not" is used are totally misunderstood by many others.

2- See Genesis 10:4 thru 9. Printed from the Old Testament. This is a contradiction with Genesis 11:1.

[4] And the sons of Javan; Elishah, and Tarshish, Kittim, and Dodanim.

[5] By these were the isles of the Gentiles divided in their lands; **every one after his tongue, after their families,** in their nations.

3- See Genesis 11:1. Thru 8. Printed from the Old Testament. This is a contradiction with Genesis 10:5 above.

[1] **And the whole earth was of one language, and of one speech.**

[2] And it came to pass, as they journeyed from the east, that they found a plain in the land of Shinar; and they dwelt there.

³And they said one to another, Go to, let us make brick, and burn them thoroughly. And they had brick for stone, and slime had they for morter.

⁴And they said, Go to, let us build us a city and a tower, whose top may reach unto heaven; and let us make us a name, lest we be scattered abroad upon the face of the whole earth.

⁵And the LORD came down to see the city and the tower, which the children of men builded.

⁶And the LORD said, Behold, the people is one, and **they have all one language**; and this they begin to do: and now nothing will be restrained from them, which they have imagined to do.

⁷Go to, let us go down, and there confound their language, that they may not understand one another's speech.

⁸So the LORD scattered them abroad from thence upon the face of all the earth: and they left off building the city.

⁹Therefore is the name of it called Babel; because the LORD did there confound the language of all the earth: and from thence did the LORD scatter them abroad upon the face of all the earth.

Frankly, I don't believe that any God of mine would stop any building and dismantle it and fling its workers to different parts of the globe just because we were trying to build something unless he/she is terrible demented himself/herself and with none loving attitudes.

There are two major contradictions that say the opposite. There are many contradictions in the King James Holy Bible but here are two very glaring examples. Not a work of a God to print theses words. Sounds like a human interpretation of a weird dream by a demented person. We have successful language interpreters now. So what's the difference? It sounds like a human statement twisting the ideas and words of this project failure to blame it on a God. In Moses day, the building engineering was not developed at all. Many places we know that humans lived in caves. Less rent to pay. If one could just keep the insects and flying birds and animals under control. One had it made instead of no comfortable place to lay your head at all. One prime example was used to tell us about cave dwelling was in Lot's story with his two daughters.

4- See Genesis 19:30 Printed from the Old Testament.

> [30]And Lot went up out of Zoar, and dwelt in the mountain, and his two daughters with him; for he feared to dwell in Zoar: and **he dwelt in a cave, he and his two daughters.**

The major reason so many names were changed in the Bible, in the Old Testament and in the New Testament as well was because of Numerology. The Bible never explains this frequent practice. Each letter represented a number. When one adds up all the letters in a name, that number might fall unlucky by its added numbers.

Change only at least one letter to make the added result come out to be a favorable name number.

1	2	3	4	5	6	7	8	9
A	B	C	D	E	F	G	H	I
J	K	L	M	N	O	P	Q	R
S	T	U	V	W	X	Y	Z	

The chart above list the number (in the Top row only)

That is assigned to each English alphabet letter seen below that number...

Some Biblical names which were changed are listed below.

Jesus —— The name of a city changed to Jebus.
Sarai —— The name of Abraham's wife to Sarah.
    Abram — the name of Sarai's husband to Abraham.
    Jacob — The name one of the Rebekah's twins to Israel.
    Joseph—the Dreamer.

Given to Pharaoh as slave, Renamed to Zaphenath-Paneah.

Also four vegetarian persons in the book of Daniel were renamed.

Who begins the Slave Market in Egypt on a big scale?
    Joseph begins and used this Slave Market himself. He was sold into slavery as a young boy by his brothers.

5- See Genesis 47:17 thru 21. Printed from the Old Testament.

[17] And they brought their cattle unto Joseph: and Joseph gave them bread in exchange for horses, and for the flocks, and for the cattle of the herds, and for the asses: and he fed them with bread for all their cattle for that year.

[18] When that year was ended, they came unto him the second year, and said unto him, we will not hide it from my lord, how that our money is spent; my lord also hath our herds of cattle; there is not ought left in the sight of my lord, **but our bodies, and our lands:**

[19] Wherefore shall we die before thine eyes, both we and our land? **Buy us and our land for bread, and we and our land will be servants unto Pharaoh:** and give us seed, that we may live, and not die, that the land be not desolate.

[20] And Joseph bought all the land of Egypt for Pharaoh; for the Egyptians sold every man his field, because the famine prevailed over them: so the land became Pharaoh's.

[21] **And as for the people, he removed them to cities** from one end of the borders of Egypt even to the other end thereof.

Joseph made the people slaves from one end of Egypt to the other. That is no mystery but what is unbelievable is that God did not intervene and allowed it to go on for not 33 years which is one generation. Not even stop it after 3 generations but didn't send someone like Moses until after 13 generations. (430 years long to be in Slavery). Frankly, I don't even believe that a God sent Moses then. Moses grew up in Pharaoh's Palace and knew his way around the Slaves. How awful, another stupid thing to do, ignore your Earth children and just let them continue to suffer. Very inconsiderate, not loving and not caring. No God Intervention! Actually when Moses story was told about freeing these slaves. They were not free yet, just changed jobs and told that they would wonder in the desert for 40 years until they died.

Some major beginning stories in the Bible.

> 6- See Genesis 3:14 Printed from the Old Testament.
> God placed a curse on the Serpent.
> God placed a curse on his supposed to be his first woman he created.
> God placed a curse on his supposed to be his first man he created.
> God placed a curse on his supposed to be his first Land he created.
> God placed a curse on his supposed to be his first off-spring he created (Cain).
> God placed a curse on anyone who kills Cain.
>
> [14]And the LORD God said unto **the serpent,** Because thou hast done this, **thou art cursed above all cattle, and above every beast of the field;** upon

thy belly shalt thou go, and dust shalt thou eat all the days of thy life:

¹⁵And I will put enmity between thee and the woman, and between thy seed and her seed; it shall bruise thy head, and thou shalt bruise his heel.

¹⁶Unto the woman he said, **I will greatly multiply thy sorrow and thy conception; in sorrow thou shalt bring forth children;** and thy desire shall be to thy husband, and he shall rule over thee.

¹⁷And unto Adam he said, because thou hast hearkened unto the voice of thy wife, and hast eaten of the tree, of which I commanded thee, saying, Thou shalt not eat of it: **cursed is the ground for thy sake; in sorrow shalt thou eat of it all the days of thy life;**

7- See Genesis 4:11 Printed from the Old Testament.

> ¹¹And **now art thou cursed from the earth**, which hath opened her mouth to receive thy brother's blood from thy hand;
>
> ¹²When thou tillest the ground, it shall not henceforth yield unto thee her strength; **a fugitive and a vagabond shalt thou be in the earth.**
>
> ¹³And Cain said unto the LORD, My punishment is greater than I can bear.

¹⁴Behold, thou hast driven me out this day from the face of the earth; and from thy face shall I be hid; and I shall be a fugitive and a vagabond in the earth; and it shall come to pass, that every one that findeth me shall slay me.

¹⁵And the LORD said unto him, therefore **whosoever slayeth Cain, vengeance shall be taken on him sevenfold.** And the LORD set a mark upon Cain, lest any finding him should kill him.

8- See Genesis 4:17 Printed from the Old Testament.

¹⁷**And Cain knew his wife**; and she conceived, and bare Enoch: and he builded a city, and called the name of the city, after the name of his son, Enoch.

Cain made love to his wife. No one knows who she was, nor where she was from. Remember Cain was supposed to be the first son born on the Earth to Adam and Eve. So his wife wasn't his mother. His wife was not his sister. Was it a monkey or other animal? I don't think so. All readers of the Bible does not know. This writer of this book knows the answer. Follow along and I will explain.

Frankly, I think that a quite possible solution to this mystery lays in a verse later in the same Genesis Book. Please be patient and follow along with me.

9- See Genesis 6:4 Printed from the Old Testament.

¹And it came to pass, when men began to multiply on the face of the earth, and daughters were born unto them,

²That **the sons of God saw the daughters of men** that they were fair; and **they took them wives of all which they chose.**

³And the LORD said, my spirit shall not always strive with man, for that he also is flesh: yet **his days shall be an hundred and twenty years.**

⁴**There were giants in the earth in those days**; and also after that, **when the sons of God came in unto the daughters of men,** and they bare children to them, the same became mighty men which were of old, men of renown.

The Nephilin were on the Earth in those days. That was when the Sons of God went to daughters of men and had children by them. The Nephilin were giants and also Heroes of long ago. They were famous men. The Nephilin were also on the Earth later on. The statement Heroes of long ago tells us that Adam and Eve were not the first created humans. It was long ago before the special creation of an experiment of Adam and Eve in the special Garden of Eden. (It did not work out as planned). The reasons for the two trees were for the Nephilin's later to be brought into this same garden. They were already off-springs from God and could be easily being granted knowledge of right and wrong plus eternal life. But God's impatience and not care continually attitude with detail caused him to get very angry with mere man and woman in his new type of human he created. So the male Father God with impatience, not loving curses were dished out very cruelly to all, the Serpent, the garden's first woman, the garden's first man and also to the Earth. That's about all as they received curses except the sky and planets. It's one of those rainy days when God got up from the wrong side of his resting place and caused a lot of havoc. Sounds like our fathers on Earth, jumping to conclusion and got to many things on his mind to handle properly with love. (I am not saying all men on Earth are like this). God did that often, causing a lot of Havoc. Again when he chose to drown every living creature on Earth with the huge deep flood. Since he was God, there was no need to do that in such a grand large scale as he was supposingly been able to accomplish a flood which was needless. One particular reason for killing them all is that he said many of them were doing the things he hates like having sex with the same sex. He could have accomplished better results by affecting their DNA and health instead. (But Moses did not know anything about DNA so his story of what God said was all his own thoughts and not words from God). Further proof that Moses was a fake when he said he talked with God daily but delivered nothing important.

God appears to have lost his temper again and again throughout the Old Testament. The fourth time was after he issued the ten commands on the stone tablets which were given to Moses, not once but twice. One of those commanding orders as a commandant was "Thou shall not commit MURDER". But he told Moses to get a big army of fighting men together and ready with swords proficient to fight for the land he had promised them. Later the Lord, God supposingly told Moses to tell the fighting men to kill hundreds and hundreds and thousands upon thousands of distant land owners and also their wives and all their children and all their Livestock, everything that breathed to get the land.

Some lands the Israel fighting people visited to take over their own land later were issued orders that they could save, not kill any females that had not made love to by a man. (Virgins). To count them when they brought them back to their own camp and divide them up as prizes to all tribes. Even the Levi priest got a share of these young Virgins.

How distasteful, the whole war, violence and killing of innocent Human Beings, Children, and animals. How awful this whole idea by a mad man named Moses.

Back near 1988, a Dictator of Iraq, which was named Saddam Hussein, ordered a troupe of spies to go check out Kuwait. (A nearby city) They did and returned home after several weeks of careful spying and examining all and documenting. Then after listening to their report, Saddam sent troupes to raid Kuwait and take possession of their land, People's oil, Finances, and anything of value which they could. He says his God Allah had given him. The troupes killed many and took several hostages and much Gold and Financial assets. Saddam says his God Allah had given the land over to him but he had to kill many first. It's a good thing the

USA and their allies went and rescued Kuwait from the jaws and clutches of Saddam Hussein about the year of 1991. It helped the innocent people of Kuwait to get some of their land and assets back to control.

At that same time, Saddam Hussein did sneak some of his men into the Kuwait oil fields and set them all afire. Dozens of them. The USA and some of their allies worked long hard days around the clock for many months to get all the oil field fires put out. The oil wells had been uncapped and set ablaze, afire. Later the USA military found in one of Saddam's many Palaces in Iraq, papers where Saddam had written the next chapter group after Moses and Joshua's Bible events where Saddam had been promised the land of Kuwait as he successfully captured and held it for several days.

10- See Leviticus 1:9 Printed from the Old Testament.

> [9]But his inwards and his legs shall he wash in water: and the priest shall burn all on the altar, to be a burnt sacrifice, **an offering made by fire, of a sweet savour unto the LORD.**

This smell of animal flesh burning was pleasant to Moses because He would have never done this daily for 40 years if he didn't enjoy the smell.

"It gives a smell that is pleasant to the Lord". Moses said. These above words are printed very similar in several of the first books of the Old Testament, many times. These same similar words are never seen printed in the New Testament. It means that as times advanced, killing animals for sacrifice was no longer needed. (Thank goodness something started by Moses could be discontinued). I think he made it up anyway. He knew that he had to feed over a million slaves daily in his army and he needed meat to solve their diet needs. He killed Bulls, lambs, pigeons, rams, and goats as sacrifices daily and as human feed. Each day for over 40 years.

Some of the slaves were back in Egypt as vegetarians but not once they started the long desert trip. There was nothing else to eat.

Think of their daily diet. Meat and Mama Crystals gathered from the ground as dew in the mornings.

11- See Leviticus 16:34 Printed from the Old Testament.

> [34]**And this shall be an everlasting statute unto you,** to **make an atonement for the children of Israel for all their sins once a year.** And he did as the LORD commanded Moses.
>
> **You must do it for all time to come. It will last forever.** Notice the statement only applied when it was first written to the children of Israel. I do not believe that the Lord ever commanded Moses like it says. I firmly believe all that God had to say thru Moses was all made up by Moses. God did not ever talk to others. That's strange in itself, a perfect setup to pretend a God was on your side. Other things I see leads to that type of conclusion. It will be revealed in my book.

12- See Luke 12:51 thru 53. Printed from the Old Testament.

[51]Suppose ye that I am come to give peace on earth? I tell you, **Nay; but rather division:**

[52]For from henceforth there shall be **five in one house divided, three against two, and two against three.**

[53]**The father shall be divided against the son, and the son against the father; the mother against the daughter, and the daughter against the mother; the mother in law against her daughter in law, and the daughter in law against her mother in law.**

Definitely not a Peace Loving Savior. What we have read is meanness, quick tempered, none respect for his relatives and mother included. A great surprise indeed.

Professor Roy Yonce's special book
PRAYER

I pray that the almighty God in heaven will see fit to grant me my following request in the Holy Name of Jesus Christ. Based on his promise in: John 14:12 thru 13."I will do anything you ask in my name".

First, I want to thank him for the nice long life he has been so kind to grant me thus far and I do hope I will be completely healthy and capable to see many more years of sun-rises and beautiful sun-sets, to share them with my loved ones.

I want to thank him also for generating within me the Research ability and close inspection capability to make very fine and meaningful, teaching and comprehensive Documents which I have been able to do for many years, as a private industry teacher working for many major fortune 500 companies, and also my years as a college Professor as well as a Licensed Commercial Pilot, also as a special Department of Defense Instructor. I thank you. (At least the last 100 times I have flown up around the clouds. I have always been able to return on the runway safely). I thank him.

I often look at others with much worse problems than I and say to myself, there goes I, but only by the grace of God. I thank him. All my thousands of students I have taught, I have tried to be motivational and fair with being a good example.

I want to do as the Mormon followers do. I am not a Mormon but have always thought it was a terrific idea, to pray and say kind wishes for your passed on relatives and friends who are lying in the grave and apparently can't help themselves.

Dear God, Please have much more mercy for all mankind and all those you killed in anger and being so quick tempered to take their lives as mentioned in so many dozens of times and places throughout the Old Testament Bible. The great world floods, the many curses placed by you on so many of your creations, the results of the Israel slave army. I thank you! For the renewed patience attempted.

Please help those to be given a better chance which was a member of Israel's marching 40 years over ½ million war party. Also a special consideration to all their victims which were in the millions which their lands, life and liberty was snuffed out so quickly because you had claimed they did sin.

I know that History has it according to the Bible; the Old Testament said that Solomon was your wisest person. It sounds not to be so, with over a thousand female personal mates. 700 choice wives, 300 concubines along with many other close female friends and servants that awesome responsibility of food, clothes, shelter and human satisfaction would make anyone lose their mind.

Even Abraham had more than one wife and had children by several other females, his wife's servants also. A very strange entanglement but yet not want to claim them as his children.

In your earlier Old Testament, you allowed Joseph to become a major slave buyer and owner of the whole Egypt's territory for Pharaoh, What a disgrace to sanction Slave ownership so widely and allow its start, and too continue for so long with people suffering.

I can remember as a little tiny young boy seeing my relatives feeding and whipping their slaves as they took me with them to the chicken house to feed their then locked up slaves. What a terrible disgrace to see their treatments and you apparently did nothing about it right away. No justice then of ever being swift at all. Those slaves died later of continuous mistreatments and malnutrition.

I pray for some special talents to be shown and given to me. I don't personally care about knowing how to play the piano. I'll leave that to others. But I would appreciate knowing and actually performing human invisibility when I need it. Also human out of the body experiences which I could use in travelling to other distant places. Also I need an ability to call face to face any dead person. Which is really actually still living. I need to help solve so many crimes of murders where so many lives were taken. I could learn to talk to them to just ask what was the real history and who did it? I need psychic ability to see into others lives as Jesus did when needed and wanted. Also the ability to raise people from the dead. So please find me worthy of all the above prayer request and honor then soon as you can. I thank you.

I pray that my God will please have mercy on me and also each of my relatives, all presently living as well as those who have joined their fathers and buried. My children and Grandchildren.

I pray for their forgiveness to my real biological parents who gave me away when I was a tiny tot knowing that there were over a dozen children in the depression year of 1933 in our home life. Please remember and forgive my adopted parents who took me into their family and home as a cherished little boy. They taught me to drive the big farm tractor when I was in my third grade of school. Please forgive my new third father whom my real biological mother did marry as he was an expert carpenter and bee hive manager. (My step father Jones).

Please have mercy and forgive any transgressions displayed by my grandmother and grandfather Cadle, The Byrds, many aunts and uncles, cousins, sisters, brothers and close friends. Also the Keilholtz family. I do miss them all. Also my close Military friends, while I was in the U.S. Navy. Fred Waldrop and his wife in San Diego,

California. Also my close friends Doctor Wayne and his wife Darlene in South Carolina. Also my other close Doctor friend, Clifford Eckert in California.

Also, please bless all the readers of this special, closely looked at book publication. Definitely have mercy on me and each one as they try to uncover the truth to help their decisions in life to be much better on a daily, weekly and monthly cycle.

Author's Brief outline of Experience

I am a retired college Department Director and a Professor where I was in college level classes teaching and making sure of smooth meaningful Department operations. I taught 12 years Engineering Electronics and computer courses for the very latest technologies. I had to research constantly daily to be lecturing to my students what they expected to be, the best and latest delivered information.

I have been in Private Industry as a Senior Design Instructor for several fortune 500 companies doing research and teachings for such companies as: General Telephone Co., Western Union Telephone and Telegraph Co., Sperry Univac Computers, RCA, Wal-Mart Home Corporation Offices, Formation Computers, Novell Computers, Decision One International, and others for a period of about 4 years each. I have forced myself to change jobs and occupations at least every 4 years. I have enjoyed doing this, it has proved extremely rewarding where no other way could I kept myself up knowledgeable on the latest technologies available.

I have had also employment of 4 years each with TWA, TransWorld Airlines, American Airlines, also the Civil Air Patrol and the Utah Civil Defense.

I have operated a Hypnosis Prescription Licensed office in my past. I have Did a lot of lecturing, demonstrations and research but really enjoyed helping with my talent, mercy Hypnosis for mostly terminated cases to relieve their pain. I have also enjoyed Age regression research periods to help prove reincarnation for past lives for some hypnosis subjects.

I also have operated my previously owned Licensed Private detective agency where I have done adjacent state investigations. I changed to a different occupation when my 4 years expired.

I have owned my own Independent Telephone Company with a 500 square miles of desert, undeveloped assigned territory by the Public Utilities Commission Agency.

I have always all my life worked a second job, sometimes a third employment at the same time.
My college degrees are in Engineering Electronics and Technical Education which I am a natural expert at teaching any and all.

The Ten Commandments

13- See Exodus 20:3 Thru 17. Printed from the Old Testament.

³Thou shalt have **no other gods before me**. # 1.

⁴Thou shalt **not make unto thee any graven image**, or any likeness of anything that is in heaven above, or that is in the earth beneath, or that is in the water under the earth. # 10

⁵Thou shalt not bow down thyself to them, nor serve them: for I the LORD **thy God am a jealous God**, visiting the iniquity of the fathers upon the children unto the third and fourth generation of them that hate me;

⁶And **showing mercy unto thousands of them** that love me, and keep my commandments.

⁷Thou **shalt not take the name of the LORD thy God in vain**; for the LORD will not hold him guiltless that taketh his name in vain. # 2.

⁸Remember **the Sabbath day, to keep it holy.** # 3

⁹**Six days shalt thou labor**, and do all thy work:

¹⁰But **the seventh day is the Sabbath of the LORD thy God**: in it thou shalt not do any work, thou, nor thy son, nor thy daughter, thy manservant, nor thy maidservant, nor thy cattle, nor thy stranger that is within thy gates: # 4

¹¹For in six days the LORD made heaven and earth, the sea, and all that in them is, **and rested the seventh day:** wherefore **the LORD blessed the Sabbath day, and hallowed it.**

¹²**Honour thy father and thy mother**: that thy days may be long upon the land which the LORD thy God giveth thee.

¹³**Thou shalt not kill.** # 5

¹⁴**Thou shalt not commit adultery.** # 6

¹⁵**Thou shalt not steal.** # 7

¹⁶**Thou shalt not bear false witness** against thy neighbor. # 8

¹⁷Thou shalt not covet thy neighbor's house; thou shalt not covet thy neighbor's wife, nor his manservant, nor his maidservant, nor his ox, nor his ass, **nor any thing that is thy neighbor's.** # 9

14- See Genesis 3:24

²⁴So he drove out the man; and he placed at the east of the Garden of Eden **Cherubims, and a flaming sword which turned every way**, to keep the way of the tree of life.

The very first mention of a surveillance intrusion alarm

Cherubims are Heavenly protection birds that have never been seen on Earth. Here is placed the actual bird. A guard. It claws and bites to protect its assigned property.

15- See Exodus 25:18 thru 22.

¹⁸**And thou shalt make two cherubims of gold**, of beaten work shalt thou make them, in the two ends of the mercy seat. **Here is placed the pictures of the actual bird.**

¹⁹And make one cherub on the one end, and the other cherub on the other end: even of the mercy seat shall ye make the cherubims on the two ends thereof.

^{20}And the cherubims shall stretch forth their wings on high, covering the mercy seat with their wings, and their faces shall look one to another; toward the mercy seat shall the faces of the cherubims be.

^{21}And thou shalt put the mercy seat above upon the ark; and in the ark thou shalt put the testimony that I shall give thee.

^{22}And there I will meet with thee, and I will commune with thee from above the mercy seat, from between the two cherubims which are upon the ark of the testimony, of all things which I will give thee in commandment unto the children of Israel.

Most readers miss these above verses that help explain each other.

16- See Joshua 1:18

^{18}Whosoever he be that doth rebel against thy commandment, and will not hearken unto thy words in all that thou commandest him, **he shall be put to death**: only be strong and of a good courage.

Joshua was told to kill anyone who did not obey him. Just as Moses' authority was to slay anyone who did not obey.

17- See Joshua 2:1

[1] And Joshua the son of Nun sent out of Shittim two men to spy secretly, saying, Go view the land, even Jericho. And they went, and came into an harlot's house, named Rahab, and lodged there.

There was no need to send spies if a God was travelling with you in your Army. A true, real God would just communicate to you what the weaknesses were in the nearby land. He would then take over to neutralize that passage. This verse is further proof of no God in the slave Israel's army.

18- See Joshua 8:1

[1] And the LORD said unto Joshua, Fear not, neither be thou dismayed: **take all the people of war with thee,** and arise, go up to Ai: see, I have given into thy hand the king of Ai, and his people, and his city, and his land:

This verse is further proof that no God travelled with the slave Israel's army. The verse says to take the whole army to fight. The whole army manpower consisted of over a half million fighting men. Sheer overpowerment. No God did anything to help.

19- See Joshua 7:4 thru 5.

⁴So there went up thither of the people about three thousand men: and they fled before the men of Ai.

⁵And the men of Ai smote of them about thirty and six men: for they chased them from before the gate even unto Shebarim, and smote them in the going down: wherefore the hearts of the people melted, and became as water.

Here is further proof that no God helped this slave army. When 3,000 fighting men went to fight, they lost lives and had to flee. The Israel's army was out numbered.

20- See Genesis 29:32 thru 35.

³²And Leah conceived, and bare a son and **she called his name Reuben**: for she said, surely the LORD hath looked upon my affliction; now therefore my husband will love me.

³³And she conceived again, and bares a son; and said, because the LORD hath heard I was hated, he hath therefore given me this son also: and **she called his name Simeon.**

³⁴And she conceived again, and bares a son; and said, now this time will my husband be joined unto me, because I have born him three sons: therefore **was his name called Levi.**

³⁵And she conceived again, and bares a son: and she said, now will I praise the LORD: therefore **she called his name Judah**; and left bearing.

Leah was the mother of six of the 12 children whom became the 12 leaders of Israel's slave army. Four of her sons are listed above. Jacob was the father. Leah had two more sons and one daughter, Dinah later.

21- **See Genesis 30:4 thru 13.**

⁴And she gave him Bilhah her handmaid to wife: and Jacob went in unto her.

⁵And Bilhah conceived, and bare Jacob a son.

⁶And Rachel said, God hath judged me, and hath also heard my voice, and hath given me a son: therefore called **she his name Dan.**

⁷And Bilhah Rachel's maid conceived again, and bare Jacob a second son.

⁸And Rachel said, with great wrestlings have I wrestled with my sister, and I have prevailed: and **she called his name Naphtali.**

⁹When Leah saw that she had left bearing, she took Zilpah her maid, and gave her Jacob to wife.

¹⁰And Zilpah Leah's maid bare Jacob a son.

¹¹And Leah said, a troop cometh: and **she called his name Gad**.

¹²And Zilpah Leah's maid bare Jacob a second son.

¹³And Leah said, Happy am I, for the daughters will call me blessed: and **she called his name Asher**.

22- See Genesis 30:17 thru 24.

¹⁷And God hearkened unto Leah, and she conceived, and **bare Jacob the fifth son.**

¹⁸And Leah said, God hath given me my hire, because I have given my maiden to my husband: and **she called his name Issachar**.

¹⁹And Leah conceived again, and **bare Jacob the sixth son.**

²⁰And Leah said, God hath endued me with a good dowry; now will my husband dwell with me, because I have born him six sons: and **she called his name Zebulun.**

²¹And afterwards she bares a daughter, and called **her name Dinah**.

²²And God remembered Rachel, and God hearkened to her, and opened her womb.

²³And she conceived, and bares a son; and said, God hath taken away my reproach:

²⁴And **she called his name Joseph**; and said, The LORD shall add to me another son.

23- See Genesis 35:16 thru 26.

¹⁶And they journeyed from Bethel; and there was but a little way to come to Ephrath: and Rachel travailed, and **she had hard labor.**

¹⁷And it came to pass, when she was in hard labor, that the midwife said unto her, Fear not; **thou shalt have this son also.**

¹⁸And it came to pass, as her soul was in departing, (for she died) that **she called his name Benoni: but his father called him Benjamin.**

¹⁹**And Rachel died**, and was buried in the way to Ephrath, which is Bethlehem.

²⁰And Jacob set a pillar upon her grave: that is the pillar of Rachel's grave unto this day.

²¹And Israel journeyed, and spread his tent beyond the tower of Edar.

²²And it came to pass, when Israel dwelt in that land, that Reuben went and lay with Bilhah his father's

concubine: and Israel heard it. **Now the sons of Jacob were twelve:**

²³The sons of Leah; Reuben, Jacob's firstborn, and Simeon, and Levi, and Judah, and Issachar, and Zebulun:

²⁴The sons of Rachel; Joseph and Benjamin:

²⁵And the sons of Bilhah, Rachel's handmaid; Dan, and Naphtali:

²⁶And the sons of Zilpah, Leah's handmaid: Gad, and Asher: these are the sons of Jacob, which were born to him in Padanaram.

Rachel's Maidservant Bilhah Gave Jacob 2 sons, Dan and Naphtali.
Leah's Maidservant Zilpah gave Jacob 2 sons, Gad and Asher.
Jacob's wife Rachael gave Jacob 2 sons, Joseph and Benjamin.
    Jacob's wife Leah gave Jacob 6 sons, Reuben, Simeon, Levi, Judah, Issachar, and Zebulun.
Making a total of 12 sons, and 1 daughter Dinah.

24- Revelations 22:18 thru 19.

¹⁸For I testify unto every man that heareth the words of the prophecy of this book, **if any man**

shall add unto these things, God shall add unto him the plagues that are written in this book:

[19]**And if any man shall take away from the words of the book of this prophecy, God shall take away his part out of the book of life,** and out of the holy city, and from the things which are written in this book.

With these words, The Author is trying to tell the publisher and reader the seriousness of keeping all verses and letters and all its words in sequential tact. Later, I will introduce to you a new way to use the original King James Version of the Holy Bible.

If any words are changed, omitted or exchanged then the PC application program will not work to its fullest capability.

It will definitely not work as expected on any of the changed, altered from the original version of the released Holy Bible.

A second warning is published in the Holy Bible warning people to not change its words nor even any letters within.

25- See Deuteronomy 4:2

²Ye shall not add unto the word which I command you, neither shall ye diminish ought from it, that ye may keep the commandments of the LORD your God which I command you.

26- See Genesis 12:10 thru 20 the following is the printed story of how Abram loaned his wife to the king for a few nights.

⁹And Abram journeyed, going on still toward the south.

¹⁰And there was a famine in the land: and Abram went down into Egypt to sojourn there; for the famine was grievous in the land.

¹¹And it came to pass, when he was come near to enter into Egypt, that he said unto Sarai his wife, Behold now, I know that thou art a fair woman to look upon:

¹²Therefore it shall come to pass, when the Egyptians shall see thee, that they shall say, this is his wife: and they will kill me, but they will save thee alive.

¹³Say, I pray thee, thou art my sister: that it may be well with me for thy sake; and my soul shall live because of thee.

¹⁴And it came to pass, that, when Abram was come into Egypt, the Egyptians beheld the woman that she was very fair.

¹⁵**The princes also of Pharaoh saw her, and commended her before Pharaoh: and the woman was taken into Pharaoh's house.**

¹⁶And he entreated Abram well for her sake: and he had sheep, and oxen, and he asses, and menservants, and maidservants, and she asses, and camels.

¹⁷**And the LORD plagued Pharaoh and his house with great plagues because of Sarai Abram's wife.**

¹⁸And Pharaoh called Abram and said, what is this that thou hast done unto me? **Why didst thou not tell me that she was thy wife?**

¹⁹**Why saidst thou, She is my sister?** So I might have taken her to me to wife: **now therefore behold thy wife, take her, and go thy way.**

²⁰And Pharaoh commanded his men concerning him: and they sent him away, and his wife, and all that he had.

27- See Genesis 13:1 thru 2

¹And **Abram went up out of Egypt, he, and his wife**, and all that he had, and Lot with him, into the south.

²And **Abram was very rich in cattle, in silver, and in gold.**

In another version of the Bible, It says that the king rewarded him much with gold and livestock for visiting with his wife.

28- See Genesis 20:1 thru 18 this is a second story where Abraham loans his wife to a different king for a few nights.

He is rewarded much money for her return. He was made richer.

¹And Abraham journeyed from thence toward the south country, and dwelled between Kadesh and Shur, and sojourned in Gerar.

²And Abraham said of Sarah his wife, **she is my sister: and Abimelech king of Gerar sent, and took Sarah.**

³But God came to Abimelech in a dream by night, and said to him, Behold, thou art but a dead man, for

the woman which thou hast taken; for she is a man's wife.

⁴But Abimelech had not come near her: and he said, LORD, wilt thou slay also a righteous nation?

⁵Said he not unto me, **She is my sister?** And she, even she herself said, **He is my brother: in the integrity of my heart and innocency of my hands have I done this.**

⁶And God said unto him in a dream, Yea, I know that thou didst this in the integrity of thy heart; for I also withheld thee from sinning against me: therefore suffered I thee not to touch her.

⁷Now therefore restore the man his wife; for he is a prophet, and he shall pray for thee, and thou shalt live: and if thou restore her not, know thou that thou shalt surely die, thou, and all that are thine.

⁸Therefore Abimelech rose early in the morning, and called all his servants, and told all these things in their ears: and the men were sore afraid.

⁹Then Abimelech called Abraham, and said unto him, what hast thou done unto us? And what have I offended thee that thou hast brought on me and on my kingdom a great sin? Thou hast done deeds unto me that ought not to be done.

¹⁰And Abimelech said unto Abraham, What sawest thou, that thou hast done this thing?

¹¹And Abraham said, because I thought, surely the fear of God is not in this place; and they will slay me for my wife's sake.

¹²**And yet indeed she is my sister; she is the daughter of my father, but not the daughter of my mother; and she became my wife.**

¹³And it came to pass, when God caused me to wander from my father's house, that I said unto her, This is thy kindness which thou shalt shew unto me; at every place whither we shall come, say of me, He is my brother.

¹⁴**And Abimelech took sheep, and oxen, and menservants, and women servants, and gave them unto Abraham, and restored him Sarah his wife.**

¹⁵And Abimelech said, Behold, my land is before thee: dwell where it pleaseth thee.

¹⁶**And unto Sarah he said, Behold, I have given thy brother a thousand pieces of silver: behold, he is to thee a covering of the eyes, unto all that are with thee, and with all other: thus she was reproved.**

¹⁷So Abraham prayed unto God: and God healed Abimelech, and his wife, and his maidservants; and they bare children.

¹⁸For the LORD had fast closed up all the wombs of the house of Abimelech, because of Sarah Abraham's wife.

29- See Genesis 26:6 thru 16 this is the printed story of Abram's Son Isaac that had been taught by his father to loan his wife to the king a few nights and become rich.

¹And there was a famine in the land, beside the first famine that was in the days of Abraham. And **Isaac went unto Abimelech king of the Philistines unto Gerar.**

²And the LORD appeared unto him, and said, Go not down into Egypt; dwell in the land which I shall tell thee of:

³Sojourn in this land, and I will be with thee, and will bless thee; for unto thee, and unto thy seed, I will give all these countries, and I will perform the oath which I sware unto Abraham thy father;

⁴And I will make thy seed to multiply as the stars of heaven, and will give unto thy seed all these countries; and in thy seed shall all the nations of the earth be blessed;

⁵Because that Abraham obeyed my voice, and kept my charge, my commandments, my statutes, and my laws.

⁶And **Isaac dwelt in Gerar:**

⁷And the men of the place asked him of his wife; and he said **she is my sister**: for he feared to say, she is my wife; lest, said he, the men of the place should kill me for Rebekah; **because she was fair to look upon.**

⁸And it came to pass, when he had been there a long time, that **Abimelech king of the Philistines looked out at a window, and saw, and, behold, Isaac was sporting with Rebekah his wife.**

⁹And **Abimelech called Isaac, and said, Behold, of a surety she is thy wife**; and how saidst thou, She is my sister? And **Isaac said unto him, because I said, lest I die for her.**

¹⁰And Abimelech said, what is this thou hast done unto us? One of the people might lightly have lien with thy wife, and thou shouldest have brought guiltiness upon us.

¹¹And **Abimelech charged all his people, saying, He that toucheth this man or his wife shall surely be put to death.**

¹²Then Isaac sowed in that land, and received in the same year an hundredfold: and the LORD blessed him.

¹³And the man waxed great, and went forward, and grew until he became very great:

¹⁴**For he had possession of flocks, and possession of herds, and great store of servants: and the Philistines envied him.**

¹⁵For all the wells which his father's servants had digged in the days of Abraham his father, the Philistines had stopped them, and filled them with earth.

¹⁶And **Abimelech said unto Isaac, Go from us; for thou art much mightier than we.**

30- **See Genesis 19:1 thru 38 this shows the extremely bad value placed on females back in biblical times. See verse 8 what the father was willing to give his two virgin daughters away to perfect strangers in the night. No value was placed on females.**

¹And there came two angels to Sodom at even; and Lot sat in the gate of Sodom: and Lot seeing them rose up to meet them; and he bowed himself with his face toward the ground;

²And he said, Behold now, my lords, turn in, I pray you, into your servant's house, and tarry all night, and wash your feet, and ye shall rise up early, and go on your ways. And they said, nay; but we will abide in the street all night.

³And he pressed upon them greatly; and they turned in unto him, and entered into his house; and he

made them a feast, and did bake unleavened bread, and they did eat.

⁴But before they lay down, the men of the city, even the men of Sodom, compassed the house round, both old and young, all the people from every quarter:

⁵And they called unto Lot, and said unto him, where are the men which came in to thee this night? Bring them out unto us, that we may know them.

⁶And Lot went out at the door unto them, and shut the door after him,

⁷And said, I pray you, brethren, do not so wickedly.

⁸**Behold now, I have two daughters which have not known man; let me, I pray you, bring them out unto you, and do ye to them as is good in your eyes:** only unto these men do nothing; for therefore came they under the shadow of my roof.

⁹And they said, Stand back. And they said again, this one fellow came in to sojourn, and he will needs be a judge: now will we deal worse with thee, than with them. And they pressed sore upon the man, even Lot, **and came near to break the door.**

¹⁰But the men put forth their hand, and pulled Lot into the house to them, and shut to the door.

[11] And they smote the men that were at the door of the house with blindness, both small and great: so that they wearied themselves to find the door.

[12] And the men said unto Lot, Hast thou here any besides? Son in law, and thy sons, and thy daughters, and whatsoever thou hast in the city, bring them out of this place:

[13] For we will destroy this place, because the cry of them is waxen great before the face of the LORD; and the LORD hath sent us to destroy it.

[14] And Lot went out, and spake unto his sons in law, which married his daughters, and said, up, get you out of this place; for the LORD will destroy this city. But he seemed as one that mocked unto his sons in law.

[15] And when the morning arose, then the angels hastened Lot, saying, Arise, take thy wife, and thy two daughters, which are here; lest thou be consumed in the iniquity of the city.

[16] And while he lingered, the men laid hold upon his hand and upon the hand of his wife, and upon the hand of his two daughters; the LORD being merciful unto him: and they brought him forth, and set him without the city.

[17] And it came to pass, when they had brought them forth abroad, that he said, Escape for thy life; look

not behind thee, neither stay thou in all the plain; escape to the mountain, lest thou be consumed.

¹⁸And Lot said unto them, Oh, not so, my LORD:

¹⁹Behold now, thy servant hath found grace in thy sight, and thou hast magnified thy mercy, which thou hast shewed unto me in saving my life; and I cannot escape to the mountain, lest some evil take me, and I die:

²⁰Behold now, this city is near to flee unto, and it is a little one: Oh, let me escape thither, (is it not a little one?) and my soul shall live.

²¹And he said unto him, See, I have accepted thee concerning this thing also, that I will not overthrow this city, for the which thou hast spoken.

²²Haste thee, escape thither; for I cannot do anything till thou become thither. Therefore the name of the city was called Zoar.

²³The sun was risen upon the earth when Lot entered into Zoar.

²⁴Then the LORD rained upon Sodom and upon Gomorrah brimstone and fire from the LORD out of heaven;

²⁵And he overthrew those cities, and all the plain, and all the inhabitants of the cities, and that which grew upon the ground.

^{26}But his wife looked back from behind him, and she became a pillar of salt.

^{27}And Abraham gat up early in the morning to the place where he stood before the LORD:

^{28}And he looked toward Sodom and Gomorrah, and toward all the land of the plain, and beheld, and, lo, the smoke of the country went up as the smoke of a furnace.

^{29}And it came to pass, when God destroyed the cities of the plain, that God remembered Abraham, and sent Lot out of the midst of the overthrow, when he overthrew the cities in the which Lot dwelt.

^{30}**And Lot went up out of Zoar, and dwelt in the mountain, and his two daughters with him; for he feared to dwell in Zoar: and he dwelt in a cave, he and his two daughters.**

^{31}And the firstborn said unto the younger, **our father is old, and there is not a man in the earth to come in unto us after the manner of all the earth:**

^{32}Come, let us make our father drink wine, and **we will lie with him, that we may preserve seed of our father.**

^{33}And they made their father drink wine that night: and **the firstborn went in, and lay with her father; and he perceived not when she lay down, nor when she arose.**

³⁴And it came to pass on the morrow, that the firstborn said unto the younger, **Behold, I lay yesternight with my father: let us make him drink wine this night also; and go thou in, and lie with him, that we may preserve seed of our father.**

³⁵And they made their father drink wine that night also: **and the younger arose, and lay with him; and he perceived not when she lay down, nor when she arose.**

³⁶Thus were both the daughters of Lot with child by their father.

³⁷And the first born bare a son, and called his name Moab: the same is the father of the Moabites unto this day.

³⁸And the younger, she also bares a son, and called his name Benammi: the same is the father of the children of Ammon unto this day.

31- See Genesis 16:1 thru 16

¹Now Sarai Abram's wife bare him no children: and she had an handmaid, an Egyptian, whose name was Hagar.

²And Sarai said unto Abram, Behold now, the LORD hath restrained me from bearing: **I pray thee, go in unto my maid; it may be that I may**

obtain children by her. And Abram hearkened to the voice of Sarai.

³And Sarai Abram's wife took Hagar her maid the Egyptian, after Abram had dwelt ten years in the land of Canaan, and gave her to her husband Abram to be his wife.

⁴And he went in unto Hagar, and she conceived: and when she saw that she had conceived, her mistress was despised in her eyes.

⁵And Sarai said unto Abram, My wrong be upon thee: I have given my maid into thy bosom; and **when she saw that she had conceived, I was despised in her eyes: the LORD judge between me and thee.**

⁶But **Abram said unto Sarai, Behold, thy maid is in thine hand; do to her as it pleaseth thee. And when Sarai dealt hardly with her, she fled from her face.**

⁷And the angel of the LORD found her by a fountain of water in the wilderness, by the fountain in the way to Shur.

⁸And he said, Hagar, Sarai's maid, whence camest thou? and whither wilt thou go? And she said, **I flee from the face of my mistress Sarai.**

⁹And the angel of the LORD said unto her, **Return to thy mistress, and submit thyself under her hands.**

¹⁰And the angel of the LORD said unto her, I will multiply thy seed exceedingly, that it shall not be numbered for multitude.

¹¹And the angel of the LORD said unto her, **Behold, thou art with child and shalt bear a son, and shalt call his name Ishmael;** because the LORD hath heard thy affliction.

¹²And he will be a wild man; his hand will be against every man, and every man's hand against him; and he shall dwell in the presence of all his brethren.

¹³And she called the name of the LORD that spake unto her, Thou God seest me: for she said, Have I also here looked after him that seeth me?

¹⁴Wherefore the well was called Beerlahairoi; behold, it is between Kadesh and Bered.

¹⁵**And Hagar bare Abram a son: and Abram called his son's name, which Hagar bare, Ishmael.**

¹⁶**And Abram was fourscore and six years old, when Hagar bare Ishmael to Abram.**

Abram was about 46 years of age and it looks like God offered No words of wisdom, no type of psychology to make any suggestion especially

verse 6 where Sarai kicked the girl out of the house. God should have suggested that the two girls get along instead, the expecting mother was kicked out in the wild, cold to roam in the wilderness to die.

32- See Exodus 32:1 thru 35

¹And when the people saw that Moses delayed to come down out of the mount, the people gathered themselves together unto Aaron, and said unto him, **Up, make us gods, which shall go before us**; for as for this Moses, the man that brought us up out of the land of Egypt, we wot not what is become of him.

²And Aaron said unto them, Break off the golden earrings, which are in the ears of your wives, of your sons, and of your daughters, and bring them unto me.

³And all the people brake off the golden earrings which were in their ears, and brought them unto Aaron.

⁴And he received them at their hand, and fashioned it with a graving tool, after **he had made it a molten calf**: and they said, These be thy gods, O Israel, which brought thee up out of the land of Egypt.

⁵And when Aaron saw it, he built an altar before it; and Aaron made proclamation, and said, tomorrow is a feast to the LORD.

⁶And they rose up early on the morrow, and offered burnt offerings, and brought peace offerings; and the people sat down to eat and to drink, and rose up to play.

⁷And the LORD said unto Moses, Go, get thee down; for thy people, which thou broughtest out of the land of Egypt, have corrupted themselves:

⁸They have turned aside quickly out of the way which I commanded them: they have made them a molten calf, and have worshipped it, and have sacrificed thereunto, and said these be thy gods, O Israel, which have brought thee up out of the land of Egypt.

⁹And the LORD said unto Moses, **I have seen this people, and, behold, it is a stiff-necked people:**

¹⁰Now therefore let me alone, that my wrath may wax hot against them, and **that I may consume them**: and I will make of thee a great nation.

¹¹And Moses besought the LORD his God, and said, LORD, why doth thy wrath wax hot against thy people, which thou hast brought forth out of the land of Egypt with great power, and with a mighty hand?

¹²Wherefore should the Egyptians speak, and say, for mischief did he bring them out, to slay them in the mountains, and to consume them from the face of the earth? **Turn from thy fierce wrath, and repent of this evil against thy people.**

¹³Remember Abraham, Isaac, and Israel, thy servants, to whom thou swarest by thine own self, and saidst unto them, I will multiply your seed as the stars of heaven, and all this land that I have spoken of will I give unto your seed, and they shall inherit it forever.

¹⁴**And the LORD repented of the evil which he thought to do unto his people.**

¹⁵And Moses turned, and went down from the mount, and the two tables of the testimony were in his hand: the tables were written on both their sides; on the one side and on the other were they written.

¹⁶And **the tables were the work of God**, and the writing was the writing of God, graven upon the tables.

¹⁷And when Joshua heard the noise of the people as they shouted, he said unto Moses, There is a noise of war in the camp.

¹⁸And he said, it is not the voice of them that shout for mastery, neither is it the voice of them that cry for being overcome: but the noise of them that sing do I hear.

¹⁹And it came to pass, as soon as he came nigh unto the camp, that he saw the calf, and the dancing: and Moses' anger waxed hot, and **he cast the tables out of his hands, and break them beneath the mount.**

²⁰And he took the calf which they had made, and burnt it in the fire, and **ground it to powder, and strawed it upon the water, and made the children of Israel drink of it.**

²¹And Moses said unto Aaron, What did this people unto thee, that thou hast brought so great a sin upon them?

²²And Aaron said, Let not the anger of my lord wax hot: thou knowest the people, that they are set on mischief.

²³For they said unto me, Make us gods, which shall go before us: for as for this Moses, the man that brought us up out of the land of Egypt, we wot not what is become of him.

²⁴And I said unto them, whosoever hath any gold, let them break it off. So they gave it me: then I cast it into the fire, and there came out this calf.

²⁵And **when Moses saw that the people were naked**; (for Aaron had made them naked unto their shame among their enemies:)

²⁶Then Moses stood in the gate of the camp, and said, **who is on the LORD's side?** Let him come

unto me. And all the sons of Levi gathered themselves together unto him.

[27] And he said unto them, Thus saith the LORD God of Israel, **Put every man his sword by his side, and go in and out from gate to gate throughout the camp, and slay every man his brother, and every man his companion, and every man his neighbor.**

[28] **And the children of Levi did according to the word of Moses: and there fell of the people that day about three thousand men.**

[29] For Moses had said, Consecrate yourselves today to the LORD, even every man upon his son, and upon his brother; that he may bestow upon you a blessing this day.

[30] And it came to pass on the morrow, that Moses said unto the people, ye have sinned a great sin: and now I will go up unto the LORD; peradventure I shall make an atonement for your sin.

[31] And Moses returned unto the LORD, and said, Oh, this people have sinned a great sin, and have made them gods of gold.

[32] Yet now, if thou wilt forgive their sin—; and if not, blot me, I pray thee, out of thy book which thou hast written.

[33] And the LORD said unto Moses, Whosoever hath sinned against me, him will I blot out of my book.

³⁴"Therefore now go, lead the people unto the place of which I have spoken unto thee: behold, mine Angel shall go before thee: nevertheless in the day when I visit I will visit their sin upon them.

³⁵**And the LORD plagued the people**, because they made the calf, which Aaron made.

This whole sequence was handled very, very badly; a real true God would have handled this situation much better than the one reported. I don't think this was any real God saying about this ordeal. He just ordered Moses to get the guards which were his own children the Levi clan to sword to death many of the others. And Moses poisoned the people by putting the melted golden Calf remains in their drink and made them drink it.

How awful. This proves to me that Moses was only pretending that a God existed along with them in his army camp. Notice that at no time, any others could ever hear any God speak. Moses was the one ordering many of his close associates sworded, killed right then. Many others died by the poison.

3,000 people were a lot to lose after such a small incident, that should have been handled much better. It's early proof that Moses decided other's fates. Not a god at all speaking Love, repentance, forgiveness, to his human creatures he had created.

33- See Exodus 34:5 thru 21

[1] And the LORD said unto Moses, Hew thee two tables of stone like unto the first: and **I will write upon these tables the words that were in the first tables,** which thou brakest.

[2] And be ready in the morning, and come up in the morning unto Mount Sinai, and present thyself there to me in the top of the mount.

[3] **And no man shall come up with thee, neither let any man be seen throughout all the mount; neither let the flocks nor herds feed before that mount.**

[4] And he hewed two tables of stone like unto the first; and Moses rose up early in the morning, and went up unto Mount Sinai, as the LORD had commanded him, and **took in his hand the two tables of stone.**

[5] And the LORD descended in the cloud, and stood with him there, and proclaimed the name of the LORD.

[6] And the LORD passed by before him, and **proclaimed, The LORD, the LORD God, merciful and gracious, longsuffering, and abundant in goodness and truth,**

[7] **Keeping mercy for thousands, forgiving iniquity and transgression and sin, and that will by no means clear the guilty; visiting the iniquity of the**

fathers upon the children, and upon the children's children, unto the third and to the fourth generation.

⁸And Moses made haste, and bowed his head toward the earth, and worshipped.

⁹And he said, if now I have found grace in thy sight, O LORD, let my LORD, I pray thee, go among us; for it is a stiff-necked people; and pardon our iniquity and our sin, and take us for thine inheritance.

¹⁰And he said, Behold, I make a covenant: before all thy people I will do marvels, such as have not been done in all the earth, nor in any nation: and all the people among which thou art shall see the work of the LORD: for it is a terrible thing that I will do with thee.

¹¹Observe thou that which I command thee this day: behold, **I drive out before thee the Amorite, and the Canaanite, and the Hittite, and the Perizzite, and the Hivite, and the Jebusite.**

¹²Take heed to thyself, lest thou make a covenant with the inhabitants of the land whither thou goest, lest it be for a snare in the midst of thee:

¹³But ye shall destroy their altars, break their images, and cut down their groves:

¹⁴For thou shalt worship no other god: for the LORD, whose name is Jealous, is a jealous God:

¹⁵Lest thou make a covenant with the inhabitants of the land, and they go a whoring after their gods, and do sacrifice unto their gods, and one call thee, and thou eat of his sacrifice;

¹⁶And thou take of their daughters unto thy sons, and their daughters go a whoring after their gods, and make thy sons go a whoring after their gods.

¹⁷Thou shalt make thee no molten gods.

¹⁸The feast of unleavened bread shalt thou keep. Seven days thou shalt eat unleavened bread, as I commanded thee, in the time of the month Abib: for in the month Abib thou camest out from Egypt.

¹⁹All that openeth the matrix is mine; and every firstling among thy cattle, whether ox or sheep, that is male.

²⁰But the firstling of an ass thou shalt redeem with a lamb: and if thou redeem him not, then shalt thou break his neck. All the firstborn of thy sons thou shalt redeem. And none shall appear before me empty.

²¹Six days thou shalt work, **but on the seventh day thou shalt rest**: in earing time and in harvest thou shalt rest.

Verse 6 says a big mouthful that has not been seen in all the Holy Bible. He appears in all Moses way of speaking for him is hate, non loving, non forgiving, non teaching, not a God

which values his stiffnecked creatures that he created.

Helps to prove there is just no God along with the Israel's war hungry leader Moses. All the sayings supposed to be God speaking to Moses is just in Moses' head.

34- See Exodus 14:23 thru 31

²¹And **Moses stretched out his hand over the sea; and the LORD caused the sea to go back by a strong east wind all that night, and made the sea dry land, and the waters were divided.**

²²And **the children of Israel went into the midst of the sea upon the dry ground: and the waters were a wall unto them on their right hand, and on their left.**

²³And **the Egyptians pursued, and went in after them to the midst of the sea, even all Pharaoh's horses, his chariots, and his horsemen.**

²⁴And **it came to pass, that in the morning watch the LORD looked unto the host of the Egyptians through the pillar of fire and of the cloud, and troubled the host of the Egyptians,**

²⁵And **took off their chariot wheels, that they drave them heavily: so that the Egyptians said, Let us flee**

from the face of Israel; for the LORD fighteth for them against the Egyptians.

²⁶And the LORD said unto Moses, **Stretch out thine hand over the sea, that the waters may come again upon the Egyptians, upon their chariots, and upon their horsemen.**

²⁷And Moses stretched forth his hand over the sea, and the sea returned to his strength when the morning appeared; and the Egyptians fled against it; and the LORD overthrew the Egyptians in the midst of the sea.

²⁸And **the waters returned, and covered the chariots, and the horsemen, and all the host of Pharaoh that came into the sea after them; there remained not so much as one of them.**

²⁹**But the children of Israel walked upon dry land in the midst of the sea; and the waters were a wall unto them on their right hand, and on their left.**

³⁰Thus the LORD saved Israel that day out of the hand of the Egyptians; and Israel saw the Egyptians dead upon the sea shore.

³¹And Israel saw that great work which the LORD did upon the Egyptians: and the people feared the LORD, and believed the LORD, and his servant Moses.

The verse 26 and 28 told of destroying all the Egyptian horsemen and their chariots. What a shame that the God didn't allow the Israel army to have them for carrying supplies across the desert for the Israel's army for the next 40 years.

With the chariots in hand, they could have drove them back to the Egyptian town they just left and got more supplies. The whole story does not fit properly with me as I search for proof. The whole ordeal appears to me done wrong if a real true God had been present. The whole hardening of the King's heart to keep the slaves from leaving for many days sounds fishy for so long and drawn out.

PERIODS OF 40 DAYS IN THE HOLY BIBLE

Old TESTAMENTS locations listed below.

35- See Genesis 7:4

[4] For yet seven days, and **I will cause it to rain upon the earth forty days and forty nights;** and every living substance that I have made will I destroy from off the face of the earth.

36- See Genesis 7:12

[12] And **the rain was upon the earth forty days and forty nights.**

37- See Genesis 7:17

[17] And **the flood was forty days upon the earth;** and the waters increased, and bare up the ark, and it was lift up above the earth.

38- See Genesis 8:6

⁶And **it came to pass at the end of forty days**, that Noah opened the window of the ark which he had made:

39- See Genesis 50:3

³And **forty days were fulfilled for him**; for so are fulfilled the days of those which are embalmed: and the Egyptians mourned for him threescore and ten days.

40- See Exodus 24:18

¹⁸And Moses went into the midst of the cloud, and gat him up into the mount: and **Moses was in the mount forty days and forty nights.**

41- See Numbers 13:25

²⁵And **they returned from searching of the land after forty days.** (Spies)

42- See Numbers 14:34

³⁴After the number of the days in which ye searched the land, **even forty days**, each day for a year, shall ye bear your iniquities, even forty years, and ye shall know my breach of promise.

43- See Deuteronomy 9:9

⁹When I was gone up into the mount to receive the tables of stone, even the tables of the covenant which the LORD made with you, then **I abode in the mount forty days and forty nights**, I neither did eat bread nor drink water:

44- See Deuteronomy 9:11

¹¹And it came to pass **at the end of forty days and forty nights**, that the LORD gave me the two tables of stone, even the tables of the covenant.

45- See Deuteronomy 9:18

¹⁸And I fell down before the LORD, as at the first, **forty days and forty nights**: I did neither eat bread, nor drink water, because of all your sins which ye sinned, in doing wickedly in the sight of the LORD, to provoke him to anger.

46- See Deuteronomy 9:25

²⁵Thus I fell down before the LORD **forty days and forty nights**, as I fell down at the first; because the LORD had said he would destroy you.

47- See Deuteronomy 10:10

¹⁰And I stayed in the mount, according to the first time, **forty days and forty nights**; and the LORD

hearkened unto me at that time also, and the LORD would not destroy thee.

48- See Mathew 4:2

^{2}And when **he had fasted forty days and forty nights**, he was afterward an hungred.

49- See Mark 1:13

^{13}And he was there in **the wilderness forty days**, tempted of Satan; and was with the wild beasts; and the angels ministered unto him.

50- See Luke 4:2

^{2}**Being forty days tempted of the devil.** And in those days he did eat nothing: and when they were ended, he afterward hungered.

51- See Acts 1:3

^{3}To whom also he shewed himself alive after his passion by many infallible proofs, **being seen of them forty days**, and speaking of the things pertaining to the kingdom of God:

52- See Numbers 1:1 thru 4 Amount of fighting men. 1st count. Also verse 18 thru 54.

^{1}And the LORD spake unto Moses **in the wilderness of Sinai**, in the tabernacle of the congregation, **on the first day of the second month, in the** second year after they were come out of the land of Egypt, saying,

²Take ye the sum of all the congregation of the children of Israel, after their families, by the house of their fathers, with the number of their names, every male by their polls;

³From twenty years old and upward, all that are able to go forth to war in Israel: thou and Aaron shall number them by their armies.

⁴And with you there shall be a man of every tribe; every one head of the house of his fathers.

¹⁸And they assembled all the congregation together on the first day of the second month, and they declared their pedigrees after their families, by the house of their fathers, according to the number of the names, from twenty years old and upward, by their polls.

¹⁹As the LORD commanded Moses, so he numbered them in the wilderness of Sinai.

²⁰And the children of Reuben, Israel's eldest son, by their generations, after their families, by the house of their fathers, according to the number of the names, by their polls, **every male from twenty years old and upward, all that were able to go forth to war;**

²¹Those that were numbered of them, even of **the tribe of Reuben, were forty and six thousand and five hundred.**

²²Of the children of Simeon, by their generations, after their families, by the house of their fathers, those that were numbered of them, according to the number of the names, by their polls, every male from twenty years old and upward, all that were able to go forth to war;

²³Those that were numbered of them, even of **the tribe of Simeon, were fifty and nine thousand and three hundred.**

²⁴Of the children of Gad, by their generations, after their families, by the house of their fathers, according to the number of the names, from twenty years old and upward, all that were able to go forth to war;

²⁵Those that were numbered of them, even of **the tribe of Gad, were forty and five thousand six hundred and fifty.**

²⁶Of the children of Judah, by their generations, after their families, by the house of their fathers, according to the number of the names, from twenty years old and upward, all that were able to go forth to war;

²⁷Those that were numbered of them, even of **the tribe of Judah, were threescore and fourteen thousand and six hundred.**

²⁸Of the children of Issachar, by their generations, after their families, by the house of their fathers, according to the number of the names, from twenty years old and upward, all that were able to go forth to war;

²⁹Those that were numbered of them, even of **the tribe of Issachar, were fifty and four thousand and four hundred.**

³⁰Of the children of Zebulun, by their generations, after their families, by the house of their fathers, according to the number of the names, from twenty years old and upward, all that were able to go forth to war;

³¹Those that were numbered of them, even of **the tribe of Zebulun, were fifty and seven thousand and four hundred.**

³²Of the children of Joseph, namely, of the children of Ephraim, by their generations, after their families, by the house of their fathers, according to the number of the names, from twenty years old and upward, all that were able to go forth to war;

³³Those that were numbered of them, even of **the tribe of Ephraim, were forty thousand and five hundred.**

³⁴Of the children of Manasseh, by their generations, after their families, by the house of their fathers, according to the number of the names, from twenty

years old and upward, all that were able to go forth to war;

³⁵Those that were numbered of them, even of **the tribe of Manasseh, were thirty and two thousand and two hundred.**

³⁶Of the children of Benjamin, by their generations, after their families, by the house of their fathers, according to the number of the names, from twenty years old and upward, all that were able to go forth to war;

³⁷Those that were numbered of them, even of **the tribe of Benjamin, were thirty and five thousand and four hundred.**

³⁸Of the children of Dan, by their generations, after their families, by the house of their fathers, according to the number of the names, from twenty years old and upward, all that were able to go forth to war;

³⁹Those that were numbered of them, even of **the tribe of Dan, were threescore and two thousand and seven hundred.**

⁴⁰Of the children of Asher, by their generations, after their families, by the house of their fathers, according to the number of the names, from twenty years old and upward, all that were able to go forth to war;

⁴¹**Those that were numbered of them, even of the tribe of Asher, were forty and one thousand and five hundred.**

⁴²Of the children of Naphtali, throughout their generations, after their families, by the house of their fathers, according to the number of the names, from twenty years old and upward, all that were able to go forth to war;

⁴³Those that were numbered of them, even of **the tribe of Naphtali, were fifty and three thousand and four hundred.**

⁴⁴These are those that were numbered, which Moses and Aaron numbered, and the princes of Israel, being twelve men: each one was for the house of his fathers.

⁴⁵So were all those that were numbered of the children of Israel, by the house of their fathers, from twenty years old and upward, all that were able to go forth to war in Israel;

⁴⁶**Even all they that were numbered were six hundred thousand and three thousand and five hundred and fifty.**

⁴⁷But **the Levites after the tribe of their fathers were not numbered among them.**

⁴⁸For the LORD had spoken unto Moses, saying,

⁴⁹**Only thou shalt not number the tribe of Levi,** neither take the sum of them among the children of Israel:

⁵⁰But **thou shalt appoint the Levites over the tabernacle of testimony,** and over all the vessels thereof, and over all things that belong to it: they shall bear the tabernacle, and all the vessels thereof; and they shall minister unto it, and shall encamp round about the tabernacle.

⁵¹And when the tabernacle setteth forward, **the Levites shall take it down: and when the tabernacle is to be pitched, the Levites shall set it up: and the stranger that cometh nigh shall be put to death.**

⁵²And the children of Israel shall pitch their tents, **every man by his own camp,** and every man by his own standard, throughout their hosts.

⁵³But the Levites shall pitch round about the tabernacle of testimony, that there be no wrath upon the congregation of the children of Israel: and **the Levites shall keep the charge of the tabernacle of testimony.**

⁵⁴And the children of Israel did according to all that the LORD commanded Moses, so did they.

603,550 Total fighting men of age for war on First count.

53- See Numbers 26:1 thru 20 Amount of fighting men. 2nd count, 39 years later.

¹And it came to pass after the plague, that the LORD spake unto Moses and unto Eleazar the son of Aaron the priest, saying,

²Take the sum of all the congregation of the children of Israel, from twenty years old and upward, throughout their fathers' house, **all that are able to go to war in Israel.**

³And Moses and Eleazar the priest spake with them **in the plains of Moab by Jordan near Jericho, saying,**

⁴Take the sum of the people, **from twenty years old and upward; as the LORD commanded Moses and the children of Israel, which went forth out of the land of Egypt.**

⁵Reuben, the eldest son of Israel: the children of Reuben; Hanoch, of whom cometh the family of the Hanochites: of Pallu, the family of the Palluites:

⁶Of Hezron, the family of the Hezronites: of Carmi, the family of the Carmites.

⁷These are the families of the Reubenites: and **they that were numbered of them were forty and three thousand and seven hundred and thirty.**

⁸And the sons of Pallu; Eliab.

⁹And the sons of Eliab; Nemuel, and Dathan, and Abiram. This is that Dathan and Abiram, which were famous in the congregation, who strove against Moses and against Aaron in the company of Korah, when they strove against the LORD:

¹⁰And the earth opened her mouth, and swallowed them up together with Korah, when that company died, what time the fire devoured two hundred and fifty men: and they became a sign.

¹¹Notwithstanding the children of Korah died not.

¹²The sons of Simeon after their families: of Nemuel, the family of the Nemuelites: of Jamin, the family of the Jaminites: of Jachin, the family of the Jachinites:

¹³Of Zerah, the family of the Zarhites: of Shaul, the family of the Shaulites.

¹⁴These are the families of **the Simeonites, twenty and two thousand and two hundred.**

¹⁵The children of Gad after their families: of Zephon, the family of the Zephonites: of Haggi, the family of the Haggites: of Shuni, the family of the Shunites:

¹⁶Of Ozni, the family of the Oznites: of Eri, the family of the Erites:

¹⁷Of Arod, the family of the Arodites: of Areli, the family of the Arelites.

¹⁸These are the families of **the children of Gad according to those that were numbered of them, forty thousand and five hundred.**

¹⁹The sons of Judah were Er and Onan: and Er and Onan died in the land of Canaan.

²⁰And the sons of Judah after their families were; of Shelah, the family of the Shelanites: of Pharez, the family of the Pharzites: of Zerah, the family of the Zarhites.

²¹And the sons of Pharez were; of Hezron, the family of the Hezronites: of Hamul, the family of the Hamulites.

²²These are **the families of Judah according to those that were numbered of them, threescore and sixteen thousand and five hundred.**

²³Of the sons of Issachar after their families: of Tola, the family of the Tolaites: of Pua, the family of the Punites:

²⁴Of Jashub, the family of the Jashubites: of Shimron, the family of the Shimronites.

²⁵These are **the families of Issachar according to those that were numbered of them, threescore and four thousand and three hundred.**

²⁶Of the sons of Zebulun after their families: of Sered, the family of the Sardites: of Elon, the family

of the Elonites: of Jahleel, the family of the Jahleelites.

²⁷These are the families of **the Zebulunites according to those that were numbered of them, threescore thousand and five hundred.**

²⁸The sons of Joseph after their families were Manasseh and Ephraim.

²⁹Of the sons of Manasseh: of Machir, the family of the Machirites: and Machir begat Gilead: of Gilead come the family of the Gileadites.

³⁰These are the sons of Gilead: of Jeezer, the family of the Jeezerites: of Helek, the family of the Helekites:

³¹And of Asriel, the family of the Asrielites: and of Shechem, the family of the Shechemites:

³²And of Shemida, the family of the Shemidaites: and of Hepher, the family of the Hepherites.

³³And Zelophehad the son of Hepher had no sons, but daughters: and the names of the daughters of Zelophehad were Mahlah, and Noah, Hoglah, Milcah, and Tirzah.

³⁴These are **the families of Manasseh, and those that were numbered of them, fifty and two thousand and seven hundred.**

³⁵These are the sons of Ephraim after their families: of Shuthelah, the family of the Shuthalhites: of Becher, the family of the Bachrites: of Tahan, the family of the Tahanites.

³⁶And these are the sons of Shuthelah: of Eran, the family of the Eranites.

³⁷These are **the families of the sons of Ephraim according to those that were numbered of them, thirty and two thousand and five hundred. These are the sons of Joseph after their families.**

³⁸The sons of Benjamin after their families: of Bela, the family of the Belaites: of Ashbel, the family of the Ashbelites: of Ahiram, the family of the Ahiramites:

³⁹Of Shupham, the family of the Shuphamites: of Hupham, the family of the Huphamites.

⁴⁰And the sons of Bela were ard and Naaman: of Ard, the family of the Ardites: and of Naaman, the family of the Naamites.

⁴¹These are **the sons of Benjamin after their families: and they that were numbered of them were forty and five thousand and six hundred.**

⁴²These are the sons of Dan after their families: of Shuham, the family of the Shuhamites. These are the families of Dan after their families.

⁴³All the families of the Shuhamites, according to those that were numbered of them, were threescore and four thousand and four hundred.

⁴⁴Of the children of Asher after their families: of Jimna, the family of the Jimnites: of Jesui, the family of the Jesuites: of Beriah, the family of the Beriites.

⁴⁵Of the sons of Beriah: of Heber, the family of the Heberites: of Malchiel, the family of the Malchielites.

⁴⁶And the name of the daughter of Asher was Sarah.

⁴⁷These are **the families of the sons of Asher according to those that were numbered of them; who were fifty and three thousand and four hundred.**

⁴⁸Of the sons of Naphtali after their families: of Jahzeel, the family of theJahzeelites: of Guni, the family of the Gunites:

⁴⁹Of Jezer, the family of the Jezerites: of Shillem, the family of the Shillemites.

⁵⁰These are **the families of Naphtali according to their families: and they that were numbered of them were forty and five thousand and four hundred.**

⁵¹These were the numbered of the children of Israel, six hundred thousand and a thousand seven hundred and thirty.

⁵²And the LORD spake unto Moses, saying,

⁵³Unto these the land shall be divided for an inheritance according to the number of names.

⁵⁴To many thou shalt give the more inheritance, and to few thou shalt give the less inheritance: to every one shall his inheritance be given according to those that were numbered of him.

⁵⁵Notwithstanding the land shall be divided by lot: according to the names of the tribes of their fathers they shall inherit.

⁵⁶According to the lot shall the possession thereof be divided between many and few.

⁵⁷And these are they that were numbered of the Levites after their families: of Gershon, the family of the Gershonites: of Kohath, the family of the Kohathites: of Merari, the family of the Merarites.

⁵⁸These are the families of the Levites: the family of the Libnites, the family of the Hebronites, the family of the Mahlites, the family of the Mushites, the family of the Korathites. And Kohath begat Amram.

⁵⁹And the name of Amram's wife was Jochebed, the daughter of Levi, whom her mother bare to Levi in Egypt: and she bare unto Amram Aaron and Moses, and Miriam their sister.

⁶⁰And unto Aaron was born Nadab, and Abihu, Eleazar, and Ithamar.

⁶¹And Nadab and Abihu died, when they offered strange fire before the LORD.

⁶²**And those that were numbered of them were twenty and three thousand, all males from a month old and upward: for they were not numbered among the children of Israel**, because there was no inheritance given them among the children of Israel.

⁶³These are they that were numbered by Moses and Eleazar the priest, who numbered the children of Israel in the plains of Moab by Jordan near Jericho.

⁶⁴**But among these there was not a man of them whom Moses and Aaron the priest numbered, when they numbered the children of Israel in the wilderness of Sinai.**

⁶⁵For the LORD had said of them, **They shall surely die in the wilderness. And there was not left a man of them, save Caleb the son of Jephunneh, and Joshua the son of Nun.**

601,730 fighting men of age for war on Second count.
39 years later after First total count.
800,000 King David counted his fighting men on a third count, who could handle a sword in Israel.

500,000 fighting men in Juda counted by King David on third count.

The below count is a repeat print just for this page view totals.
603,550 Total fighting men of age for war on First count.

What do we know about Moses?

Information taken from the KJ Bible, Age Regression Hypnotic trance subjects, Psychics and the Dead Sea Scrolls.

He was born to the house of Levi, his mother was a Levi. His father Amram was a Levi. Amram lived 137 years. Moses' mother's name was Jachebed. She was Moses' father's sister. She bore both Aaron and Moses, the two sons and one daughter Mirian in incest.

Moses was given away, put in an ark to float away, down stream from the reeds by the river's bank when he was just 3 months old. A time his mother could no longer hide the beautiful nice featured little boy from the really mean Pharaoh King. This King had commanded all his people saying "Every son who is born, you shall cast into the river, and every daughter you shall save alive". The King was said to even have murdered his own son because of the Psychic news that flew around in conversation circles of a respected leader in that part of the country. At this early 3 month life age, he was watched very carefully by his older sister. Mirian to witness his fate as it floated on the river waters. Because of the King's order to throw all male babies into the river as crocodile food, It doesn't tell us, but I'm sure thousands were killed, drowned using this method, for many years. The male population of Hebrews was dwindling fast.

He was found by the maidens of the daughter of the Pharaoh as she came down to bath at the river. Mirian said to Pharaoh's daughter, an offering to get it a nurse for the child from the Hebrew women. That way, the Hebrew woman could nurse the child. So the maiden went and acquired the baby's mother, on an oral contract to nurse and breast feed the baby.

After the baby became old enough to be weaned, the child grew and was brought to the Pharaoh's daughter and became her new son. She named him Moses and he was raised as a Royal in the Palace. He lived and stayed in the Palace over 25 years . The new mother hid the new son daily from the King as it grew up in the King's Palace. Having many private tours to teach it the ways of the Palace. How to read, How to write, How to count, Secret Magicians' ways of producing things with magic. He was taught awning making, clothes making, curtain making, sewing of many kinds, melting of gold, copper, silver, other metals and how to mold anything to a solid. He was taught many dozens of talents that one learns when growing up in a King's Palace. One particular thing he suffered in his learning was how to speak to others. That was one major thing lacking in his experiences. He was often told to hide from the new grandfather, a foster relative and just exist where he could without being heard nor seen with the threat of death as his safety measure. Later after he had reached adulthood, he was forced to flee his Palace home because he was then a wanted fugitive, having killed an Egyptain man slave guard for beating a Hebrew slave, and hiding the murdered body in the sand. He was over 25 years old when he left the Palace.

He heard that he was a wanted murderer, wanted by the King for this killing. The King sought to kill Moses. So, Moses left Egypt on foot. We can pretty well assume that the Moses in growing up heard many a conversation between the King and hundreds of others plotting shameful deeds. The King was cruel, mean, vicious, greedy and to selfish to be for any good cause.

After hearing about his own story with orders to be thrown into the river as a baby, it was told to Moses many times by his foster mother, the King's daughter as his own protection against coming into direct contact with such a mean grandfather down any hallway he may walk. I'm sure that Moses has heard his share of loud talking and loud voices from the King on occasions as he would be reprimanding some civil servant of his to do a slippery deed far away from the Palace. Moses probably learned a lot about what was actually going on with the loud conversations of filled hatefulness and cruel plannings. He had his own small cubby hole to hide in at times when it was known that the King would be near this sector of the Palace.

His new mother, the King's daughter had enlisted some others to help her protect this Moses child as he slept and ate and attended his private meetings, always in the Castle or Palace for his maturing and developing Education purposes.

Very few other children to play with and always ready to be hid in a moment's notice!

He adapted quickly to his new job as a sheep herder when he took Zipporah as his wife. His secret past of always being hid in the Palace while growing up caused him more than likely to always be looking over his shoulder for any attacker while he was busy attending his father-In-Laws sheep. The open range meant fresh air and more freedom, but always on guard.

Could it have been a Delusionist experience to have seen a burning bush that did not consume in its flames? Others believe very much in the possibility under his personality and experience, especially an offspring of Incest, also a wanted murderer he had to watch every step he took.

It was easy to figure the King's life span expectancy back then, not good medicine, not a good rest period continually. Not the best balanced foods. Moses remembered hearing the King and seeing the King between parted curtains many times and listened to his hollowing. He knew the life expectancy of the King at all times and possible conditions.

You must remember along with clear writings also read by this author. Moses was the only person to be allowed anywhere on this big mountain that was supposed to be the home of God. You have even read the rules to shoot an arrow or stone to death anyone who tried to follow Moses and Joshua up this mountain, to get even any glimpse of God. No sheep herder or even any animals were allowed ever anywhere up on this mountain. Not even at the foot of the mountain. It was a mountain belonging to Moses, and to only Moses. He learned some great magic tricks to pull the wool over all those slave army people. He sat up classes for them to become marksmen at the rock slinging skill. He also set up classes for sword fighting. He remembers his King saying that those two attributes are very critical to have in a war party plus moving quietly into position.

Moses best learned and practiced talent which he mastered early in his young closet settings was record keepings which he prided himself really good at. He was a masterful practitioner of writing so others understood what his comments meant. He always liked listing items of interest since a child. He wrote many a scroll full of things to know. Sometimes when nothing could be done, Moses copied his worse scrolls into new manuscripts.

After Moses was in his thirties, Moses found a new home at the place of a Midian Priest, named Jethro. Jethro had seven daughters and liked Moses. Jethro had a son named Hobab. Jethro gave one of his daughters, Zipporah to Moses as his wife. After a few years, of being with his new wife, she had a couple of sons by Moses. Zipporah's two sons were named Gershom and Eliezer. Moses lived with her two sons and wife in Midian from about his age of 36 until he was 79 years of age. Then at this age, He made the trip to Egypt to see the Pharaoh the King and brought the slaves back from Egypt.

54- See John 1:18

[18]No man hath seen God at any time, the only begotten Son, which is in the bosom of the Father, he hath declared him.

There were references in the Bible that says many of Hebrew slaves saw God but further places contradicted that in saying, no one could ever look upon God and live. Moses was the spokesperson of anything God was supposed to have said. He related any and all important sayings and Laws and Rules from God to the people.

Abraham claimed that He saw God. Another CONTRADICTION.

There were times, when Moses treated the slaves as mere ignorant dumb slaves and said God wanted to do away with many of them. And it was reported, that God did just that. Plagues came upon the slave army and many died with no help from God. In fact, if one reads Genesis and the other 4 beginning books completely, He/She will find references that God has chosen to just let the whole army of older experienced people die during the last 40 years through staying and wandering in the desert. Only the young and new borns survived to be made into a new equipped army of fighting men to terrorize the already existing land owners of the so called promised lands.

This book is called "A closer look at the King James version Bible". But it could easily be referred to as "A closer look at the very first Authorized Terror Army Handbook".

55- See Numbers 15:32 thru 36

³²And while the children of Israel were in the wilderness, **they found a man that gathered sticks upon the Sabbath day.**

³³And **they that found him gathering sticks brought him unto Moses and Aaron, and unto all the congregation.**

³⁴And **they put him in ward, because it was not declared what should be done to him.**

³⁵And the LORD said unto Moses, **The man shall be surely put to death: all the congregation shall stone him with stones without the camp.**

³⁶And **all the congregation brought him without the camp, and stoned him with stones, and he died;** as the LORD commanded Moses.

> Thank goodness that law of lifting your fingers on Sunday does not exist today. Awful of Moses to con deem that man for such a small act he was doing. All the slave people should have told God to punish him if he claims sin against him, himself. Then the man and others later would not have died. The killing and punishments were Moses' doing alone. I am convinced.

56- See Judges 20:16

¹⁶Among all this people there were **seven hundred chosen men left-handed; every one could sling stones at an hair breadth, and not miss.**

¹⁷And the men of Israel, **beside Benjamin, were numbered four hundred thousand men that drew sword: all these were men of war.**

> The above shows much, much practice daily to get this Israel slave Army ready.

57- See Judges 21:11 thru 15 The Israel army stole 400 women for their own use. Just kidnapped them and captured all by surprise. Then they were taken completely from all love ones to their new homes after killing every previous virgin's relative they could find.

[10] And the congregation sent thither **twelve thousand men of the valiantest, and commanded them, saying, Go and smite the inhabitants of Jabeshgilead with the edge of the sword, with the women and the children.**

[11] And this is the thing that ye shall do, **Ye shall utterly destroy every male, and every woman that hath lain by man.**

[12] And **they found among the inhabitants of Jabeshgilead four hundred young virgins, that had known no man by lying with any male: and they brought them unto the camp to Shiloh, which is in the land of Canaan.**

[13] And the whole congregation sent some to speak to the children of Benjamin that were in the rock Rimmon, and to call peaceably unto them.

[14] And Benjamin came again at that time; **and they gave them wives which they had saved alive of the women of Jabeshgilead: and yet so they sufficed them not.**

¹⁵And the people repented them for Benjamin, because that the LORD had made a breach in the tribes of Israel.

¹⁶Then **the elders of the congregation said, how shall we do for wives for them that remain, seeing the women are destroyed out of Benjamin?**

¹⁷And they said, There must be an inheritance for them that be escaped of Benjamin, that a tribe be not destroyed out of Israel.

¹⁸Howbeit we may not give them wives of our daughters: for the children of Israel have sworn, saying, Cursed be he that giveth a wife to Benjamin.

¹⁹Then they said, Behold, there is a feast of the LORD in Shiloh yearly in a place which is on the north side of Bethel, on the east side of the highway that goeth up from Bethel to Shechem, and on the south of Lebonah.

²⁰Therefore they commanded the children of Benjamin, saying, Go and lie in wait in the vineyards;

²¹And see, and, behold, if **the daughters of Shiloh come out to dance in dances, then come ye out of the vineyards, and catch you every man his wife of the daughters of Shiloh, and go to the land of Benjamin.**

²²And it shall be, **when their fathers or their brethren come unto us to complain, that we will**

say unto them, **Be favourable unto them for our sakes:** because we reserved not to each man his wife in the war: for ye did not give unto them at this time, that ye should be guilty.

¹⁰ And the congregation sent thither twelve thousand men of the valiantest, and commanded them, saying, Go and smite the inhabitants of Jabeshgilead with the edge of the sword, with the women and the children.

¹¹ And this is the thing that ye shall do, Ye shall utterly destroy every male, and every woman that hath lain by man.

¹² And they found among the inhabitants of Jabeshgilead four hundred young virgins that had known no man by lying with any male: and they brought them unto the camp to Shiloh, which is in the land of Canaan.

¹³ And the whole congregation sent some to speak to the children of Benjamin that were in the rock Rimmon, and to call peaceably unto them.

¹⁴ And Benjamin came again at that time; and they gave them wives which they had saved alive of the women of Jabeshgilead: and yet so they sufficed them not.

¹⁵ And the people repented them for Benjamin, because that the LORD had made a breach in the tribes of Israel.

¹⁶Then the elders of the congregation said, how shall we do for wives for them that remain, seeing the women are destroyed out of Benjamin?

¹⁷And they said, There must be an inheritance for them that be escaped of Benjamin, that a tribe be not destroyed out of Israel.

¹⁸Howbeit we may not give them wives of our daughters: for the children of Israel have sworn, saying, Cursed be he that giveth a wife to Benjamin.

¹⁹Then they said, Behold, there is a feast of the LORD in Shiloh yearly in a place which is on the north side of Bethel, on the east side of the highway that goeth up from Bethel to Shechem, and on the south of Lebonah.

²⁰Therefore they commanded the children of Benjamin, saying, Go and lie in wait in the vineyards;

²¹And see, and, behold, if the daughters of Shiloh come out to dance in dances, then come ye out of the vineyards, and catch you every man his wife of the daughters of Shiloh, and go to the land of Benjamin.

²²And it shall be, when their fathers or their brethren come unto us to complain, that we will say unto them, Be favorable unto them for our sakes: because we reserved not to each man his wife in the war: for ye did not give unto them at this time, that ye should be guilty.

²³And the children of Benjamin did so, and took them wives, according to their number, of them that danced, whom they caught: and they went and returned unto their inheritance, and repaired the cities, and dwelt in them.

²⁴And **the children of Israel departed thence at that time, every man to his tribe and to his family,** and they went out from thence every man to his inheritance.

²⁵In those days there was no king in Israel: **every man did that which was right in his own eyes.**

, whom they caught: and they went and returned unto their inheritance, and repaired the cities, and dwelt in them.

²⁴And the children of Israel departed thence at that time, every man to his tribe and to his family, and they went out from thence every man to his inheritance.

²⁵In those days there was no king in Israel: every **man did that which was right in his own eyes.**

No King's laws, every man could do what he wanted.

They kidnapped enough young females to make enough wives.

They slipped in and caught them at a Dance.

This is treatment worse than they were treated themselves back as slaves in Egypt.

Women were not valued by their so called Moses' God, nor the Israel slave army. A terrible disgrace! It helps to prove there was no God helping them.

58- See Judges 1:21

[21] And the children of Benjamin did not drive out the Jebusites that inhabited Jerusalem; but the Jebusites dwell with the children of Benjamin in Jerusalem unto this day.

First, the City named Jesus was Jerusalem. The name was changed one letter different to make the Numerology read more positive and acceptable.

Jesus city was changed to Jebus. Now its inhabitants were called Jebusites.

This verse declares that the Israel slave army could not drive out the Jebusites. Another version of the Bible states it was because the Jebusites owned chariots.

Further proof that no God helped them because a real true God would have known how to handle any one with Chariots as the slave army did not know how to control Chariots.

59- See Luke 4:30 Here are a few verses which proves that Jesus knew and used an ability he learned which was to allow himself to become invisible when needed.

^{28}And all they in the synagogue, when they heard these things, were filled with wrath,

^{29}And rose up, and thrust him out of the city, and led him unto the brow of the hill whereon their city was built, that they might cast him down headlong.

^{30}But he passing through the midst of them went his way,

No one saw which way he travelled. They were angry enough to kill Jesus. But no one saw where he went.

60- See John 8:52 thru 68. Another verse stating he escaped their furor without being seen.

^{52}Then said the Jews unto him, now we know that thou hast a devil. Abraham is dead, and the prophets; and thou sayest, if a man keep my saying, he shall never taste of death.

^{53}Art thou greater than our father Abraham, which is dead? And the prophets are dead: whom makest thou thyself?

⁵⁴Jesus answered, if I honour myself, my honour is nothing: it is my Father that honoureth me; of whom ye say, that he is your God:

⁵⁵Yet ye have not known him; but I know him: and if I should say, I know him not, I shall be a liar like unto you: but I know him, and keep his saying.

⁵⁶Your father Abraham rejoiced to see my day: and he saw it, and was glad.

⁵⁷Then said the Jews unto him, Thou art not yet fifty years old, and hast thou seen Abraham?

⁵⁸Jesus said unto them, Verily, verily, I say unto you, Before Abraham was, I am.

⁵⁹Then took they up stones to cast at him: but Jesus hid himself, and went out of the temple, going through the midst of them, and so passed by.

He had made himself invisible again.

61- See John 10:29 thru 39.

²⁹My Father, which gave them me, is greater than all; and no man is able to pluck them out of my Father's hand.

³⁰I and my Father are one.

³¹Then the Jews took up stones again to stone him.

³²Jesus answered them, Many good works have I shewed you from my Father; for which of those works do ye stone me?

³³The Jews answered him, saying, for a good work we stone thee not; **but for blasphemy;** and because that thou, being a man, makest thyself God.

³⁴Jesus answered them, is it not written in your law, I said, Ye are gods?

³⁵If he called them gods, unto whom the word of God came, and the scripture cannot be broken;

³⁶Say ye of him, whom the Father hath sanctified, and sent into the world, Thou blasphemest; because I said, I am the Son of God?

³⁷If I do not the works of my Father, believe me not.

³⁸But if I do, though ye believe not me, believe the works: that ye may know, and believe, that the Father is in me, and I in him.

³⁹Therefore they sought again to take him: but he escaped out of their hand,

He had made himself invisible again.

62- See John 12:36.

³⁶While ye have light, believe in the light, that ye may be the children of light. These things spake Jesus, and departed, and did hide himself from them.

He had made himself invisible again.

63- See Mathew 9:4 Jesus was very psychic.

⁴**And Jesus knowing their thoughts** said, Wherefore think ye evil in your hearts?

64- See 2 Peter 3:8 God's time span is different.

⁸But, beloved, be not ignorant of this one thing, **that one day is with the Lord as a thousand years, and a thousand years as one day.**

We did four pages on the story of Moses.

Then about eight pages on Bible verses to break up any monotone.

Now, we will go back to continue the story of Moses.

Even Moses was not allowed to go up close and witness the so called promised land. Moses died and he was buried in the valley of the Land of Moab. Moses was one hundred and twenty years old when he died. Joshua had been his lifetime assistant and took over the command of this large terrorizing slave army.

The first five books of the Torah is referred to as the Pentateuch. They are told that it is the written work of Moses himself. This author says they are not even his accumulated work because of so many conflicted statements, contradictions, none continuity of facts and bold blazin statements. All could not have been his work nor even a God's work because of non consistent of truthful facts lay all throughout these five books. They are all in a different format of telling their story. (Indicating not the same person authored all).

One of the very first contradictions, It states very plainly there was only one universal language spoken. It states that was why the Babel Tower was destroyed, to create Babel instead of coherent understandings between architects. This is NONSENSE!

65- See Genesis 10:5. Printed from the Old Testament. This is a contradiction with Genesis 11:1.

[5] By these were the isles of the Gentiles divided in their lands; **every one after his tongue, after their families,** in their nations.

As not too much further, in a different group of verses, it was stated they had many different languages according to their own language in their individual land.

66- See Genesis 11:1. Printed from the Old Testament. This is a contradiction with Genesis 10:5

[1] **And the whole earth was of one language, and of one speech.**

67- **See Numbers 13:1 thru 33. This group of following verses is why the whole trip got delayed by to take 40 years, and let the adult army just die in the wandering desert. It proves that Moses was the one making all such decisions and not any God at all was with them.**

¹And the LORD spake unto Moses, saying,

²**Send thou men, that they may search the land of Canaan**, which I give unto the children of Israel: of every tribe of their fathers shall ye send a man, everyone a ruler among them.

³And Moses by the commandment of the LORD sent them from the wilderness of Paran: **all those men were heads of the children of Israel.**

⁴And these were their names: of the tribe of Reuben, Shammua the son of Zaccur.

⁵Of the tribe of Simeon, Shaphat the son of Hori.

⁶Of the tribe of Judah, Caleb the son of Jephunneh.

⁷Of the tribe of Issachar, Igal the son of Joseph.

⁸Of the tribe of Ephraim, Oshea the son of Nun.

⁹Of the tribe of Benjamin, Palti the son of Raphu.

¹⁰Of the tribe of Zebulun, Gaddiel the son of Sodi.

¹¹Of the tribe of Joseph, namely, of the tribe of Manasseh, Gaddi the son of Susi.

¹²Of the tribe of Dan, Ammiel the son of Gemalli.

¹³Of the tribe of Asher, Sethur the son of Michael.

¹⁴Of the tribe of Naphtali, Nahbi the son of Vophsi.

¹⁵Of the tribe of Gad, Geuel the son of Machi.

¹⁶These are the names of the men which **Moses sent to spy out the land**. And Moses called Oshea the son of Nun Jehoshua.

¹⁷And Moses sent them to spy out the land of Canaan, and said unto them, **Get you up this way southward, and go up into the mountain:**

¹⁸And see the land, what it is, and the people that dwelleth therein, whether **they be strong or weak, few or many;**

¹⁹And **what the land is that they dwell in, whether it be good or bad; and what cities they be that they dwell in, whether in tents, or in strong holds;**

²⁰And **what the land is, whether it be fat or lean, whether there be wood therein, or not. And be ye of good courage, and bring of the fruit of the land. Now the time was the time of the firstripe grapes.**

²¹So they went up, and searched the land from the wilderness of Zin unto Rehob, as men come to Hamath.

²²And they ascended by the south, and came unto Hebron; where Ahiman, Sheshai, and Talmai, the

children of Anak, were. (Now Hebron was built seven years before Zoan in Egypt.)

23 And they came unto the brook of Eshcol, and **cut down from thence a branch with one cluster of grapes, and they bare it between two upon a staff; and they brought of the pomegranates, and of the figs.**

24 The place was called the brook Eshcol, because of the cluster of grapes which the children of Israel cut down from thence.

25 **And they returned from searching of the land after forty days.**

26 And **they went and came to Moses, and to Aaron, and to all the congregation of the children of Israel, unto the wilderness of Paran, to Kadesh; and brought back word unto them, and unto all the congregation, and shewed them the fruit of the land.**

27 And **they told him, and said, We came unto the land whither thou sentest us, and surely it floweth with milk and honey; and this is the fruit of it.**

28 Nevertheless **the people be strong that dwell in the land, and the cities are walled, and very great: and moreover we saw the children of Anak there.**

²⁹The Amalekites dwell in the land of the south: and the Hittites, and the Jebusites, and the Amorites, dwell in the mountains: and the Canaanites dwell by the sea, and by the coast of Jordan.

³⁰And Caleb stilled the people before Moses, and said, Let us go up at once, and possess it; for we are well able to overcome it.

³¹**But the men that went up with him said, We be not able to go up against the people; for they are stronger than we.**

³²And they brought up an evil report of the land which they had searched unto the children of Israel, saying, **The land, through which we have gone to search it, is a land that eateth up the inhabitants thereof; and all the people that we saw in it are men of a great stature.**

³³**And there we saw the giants, the sons of Anak, which come of the giants: and we were in our own sight as grasshoppers, and so we were in their sight.**

You need to study this over and over to see just what exactly happened. Because Moses said they lied about this trip and Moses said they made a false report. I do not agree. The report looks very honest indeed. Moses got so mad that he said 40 more years are needed to let all the people who went on the spy trip to die. Moses thought he would have less resistance to this war he wanted if he raised the young babies which would be born later better himself. Otherwise a better Brainwashing. Besides, the fact that if a real true God was in their camp helping the army as Moses said all along, That God would have handled this mess much better than Moses did.

This group of verses starting at Numbers 13:1 gives evidence about a big mix-up in the Leaders and Moses of the Hebrew Terror army and so called anger of God.

It appears that these verses tells about Moses sending a qualified leaders group of well experienced men to spy out this new promised land of Canaan. Each man chosen to be a spy was rightly a mighty leader with great judgement and ability. One leader was chosen from each of the 12 groups plus Joshua to go on a 40 day expedition to gather info all about this land and its people to report back its findings.

God was supposed to have spoken to Moss and ordered this Spy hunt for further details about the actual fact findings of their promised land.

1- To see just exactly just what the land is like.

2- Whether the people who dwell in it are strong or weak.

3- Whether the people are few or many.

4- Whether the land is good or bad.

5- Whether the cities they inhabit are like camps or strongholds.

6- Whether the land is rich or poor.

7- Whether there are forests or not.

8- To bring some fruits back from the land in the season of grapes.

They returned after spying for 40 days, bringing plenty of different kinds of fruit.

IS IT NOT STRANGE INDEED THAT THEIR TAG ALONG GOD DID NOT KNOW THESE 8 ANSWERS AND PROVIDE ALL NEEDED INFO AHEAD OF ANY SUCH TRIP?

The story in these actual verses discloses for the very first time, that Moses got very mad and disliked such a report that didn't have men that would be ready for all out war and killings. It was the very first time it was revealed that the whole army had to pass thoughts of MURDER and TERROR toward the old owners of this promised land to become it's new inhabitants and owners. At this point, It is very accurate to state that this was Moses plan all along to just simply kill and murder all the people and take it over as their captured land.

Do it in the name of ALLAH saying God was even with them in their army and on their side. (The slaves were too dumb to know any better).

Other ruthless, mean and not loving leaders has had the very same vicious plans also throughout history.

The ones and major verses are the ones where Moses is caught lying and falsifying the records saying they are supposed to be God's words himself.

68- See Numbers 14:1 thru 45.

¹And all the congregation lifted up their voice, and cried; and the people wept that night.

²And all the children of Israel murmured against Moses and against Aaron: and the whole congregation said unto them, Would God that we had died in the land of Egypt! or would God we had died in this wilderness!

³And wherefore hath the LORD brought us unto this land, to fall by the sword, that our wives and our children should be a prey? were it not better for us to return into Egypt?

⁴**And they said one to another, Let us make a captain, and let us return into Egypt.**

⁵Then Moses and Aaron fell on their faces before all the assembly of the congregation of the children of Israel.

⁶And Joshua the son of Nun, and Caleb the son of Jephunneh, which were of them that searched the land, rent their clothes:

⁷And they spake unto all the company of the children of Israel, saying, The land, which we passed through to search it, is an exceeding good land.

⁸If the LORD delight in us, then he will bring us into this land, and give it us; a land which floweth with milk and honey.

⁹Only rebel not ye against the LORD, **neither fear ye the people of the land; for they are bread for us: their defence is departed from them, and the LORD is with us: fear them not.**

¹⁰But **all the congregation bade stone them with stones**. And the glory of the LORD appeared in the tabernacle of the congregation before all the children of Israel.

¹¹And the LORD said unto Moses, How long will this people provoke me? and how long will it be ere they believe me, for all the signs which I have shewed among them?

¹²I will smite them with the pestilence, and disinherit them, and will make of thee a greater nation and mightier than they.

¹³And Moses said unto the LORD, Then the Egyptians shall hear it, (for thou broughtest up this people in thy might from among them;)

¹⁴And they will tell it to the inhabitants of this land: for they have heard that thou LORD art among this people, that thou LORD art seen face to face, and that thy cloud standeth over them, and that thou goest before them, by day time in a pillar of a cloud, and in a pillar of fire by night.

¹⁵Now if thou shalt kill all this people as one man, then the nations which have heard the fame of thee will speak, saying,

¹⁶Because the LORD was not able to bring this people into the land which he sware unto them, therefore he hath slain them in the wilderness.

¹⁷And now, I beseech thee, let the power of my lord be great, according as thou hast spoken, saying,

¹⁸The LORD is longsuffering, and of great mercy, forgiving iniquity and transgression, and by no means clearing the guilty, visiting the iniquity of the fathers upon the children unto the third and fourth generation.

[19] Pardon, I beseech thee, the iniquity of this people according unto the greatness of thy mercy, and as thou hast forgiven this people, from Egypt even until now.

[20] And the LORD said, I have pardoned according to thy word:

[21] But as truly as I live, all the earth shall be filled with the glory of the LORD.

[22] Because all those men which have seen my glory, and my miracles, which I did in Egypt and in the wilderness, and have tempted me now these ten times, and have not hearkened to my voice;

[23] **Surely they shall not see the land which I sware unto their fathers, neither shall any of them that provoked me see it:**

[24] But my servant Caleb, because he had another spirit with him, and hath followed me fully, him will I bring into the land whereinto he went; and his seed shall possess it.

[25] (Now the Amalekites and the Canaanites dwelt in the valley.) Tomorrow turn you, and get you into the wilderness by the way of the Red sea.

[26] And the **LORD** spake unto Moses and unto Aaron, saying,

^{27}How long shall I bear with this evil congregation, which murmur against me? **I have heard the murmurings of the children of Israel, which they murmur against me.**

^{28}Say unto them, As truly as I live, saith the LORD, as ye have spoken in mine ears, so will I do to you:

^{29}Your carcases shall fall in this wilderness; and all that were numbered of you, according to your whole number, from twenty years old and upward which have murmured against me.

^{30}Doubtless ye shall not come into the land, concerning which I sware to make you dwell therein, save Caleb the son of Jephunneh, and Joshua the son of Nun.

^{31}But your little ones, which ye said should be a prey, them will I bring in, and they shall know the land which ye have despised.

^{32}But as for you, your carcases, they shall fall in this wilderness.

^{33}And your children shall wander in the wilderness forty years, and bear your whoredoms, until your carcases be wasted in the wilderness.

^{34}After the number of the days in which ye searched the land, even forty days, each day for a year, shall ye bear your iniquities, even forty years, and ye shall know my breach of promise.

³⁵I the LORD have said, I will surely do it unto all this evil congregation, that are gathered together against me: in this wilderness they shall be consumed, and there they shall die.

³⁶And the men, which Moses sent to search the land, who returned, and made all the congregation to murmur against him, by bringing up a slander upon the land,

³⁷Even those men that did bring up the evil report upon the land, died by the plague before the LORD.

³⁸But Joshua the son of Nun, and Caleb the son of Jephunneh, which were of the men that went to search the land, lived still.

³⁹And **Moses told these sayings unto all the children of Israel**: and the people mourned greatly.

⁴⁰And they rose up early in the morning, and gat them up into the top of the mountain, saying, Lo, we be here, and will go up unto the place which the LORD hath promised: for we have sinned.

⁴¹And Moses said, Wherefore now do ye transgress the commandment of the LORD? but it shall not prosper.

⁴²**Go not up, for the LORD is not among you;** that ye be not smitten before your enemies.

^{43}For the Amalekites and the Canaanites are there before you, and ye shall fall by the sword: because ye are turned away from the LORD, therefore the LORD will not be with you.

^{44}But they presumed to go up unto the hill top: nevertheless the ark of the covenant of the LORD, and Moses, departed not out of the camp.

^{45}Then the Amalekites came down, and the Canaanites which dwelt in that hill, and smote them, and discomfited them, even unto Hormah.

> Moses got all the true fact all distorted here and accused all the Spies of wrong doings and just proclaimed that all would die except a couple. (Caleb and Joshua) Here seen above, Moses decides to just let them roam and wander in the desert to die of plagues.
>
> It is more than lightly his plan to feed them more tainted drinks to give them some plagues. He would make sure the adults all would die, just like he did when they were made to drink the melted gold during the golden calf situation earlier.
>
> A terrible shame. All the evidence against their own chosen spies did not warrant this type of treatment from Moses. Further proof that there was no God with the Israel slave army on their trip. One of the reasons Moses de-

cided to wait many years to run on them again is because verse **44** and **45** above got all the enemies stirred up and alerted as they would know about any surprise attacks and would be watching for them to be coming over the hill.

Verse 10 above had Moses doing some of his magician's magic here pulling the wool over the eyes of the slaves again proclaiming that God was with them.

69- See Joshua 8:1

[1]And the LORD said unto Joshua, Fear not, neither be thou dismayed: **take all the people of war with thee,** and arise, go up to Ai: see, I have given into thy hand the king of Ai, and his people, and his city, and his land:

The above verses are further proof that no God exist with them as Moses says take the whole entire army and take with a war, their land. All their war army people is over half a million in size. Pure outnumbered group and so what if a few thousand Israel slaves gets killed in the process, like they did in verse **45**. Moses can't stand some of those stiff-necked people anyway.

"Thou shall not murder" Command, it was to just be thrown away in the trash.

"Thou shall not covet their neighbor's things". Until the new land was captured, disregard it also. Moses tried to convince all slaves that God was travelling with them in their army, He understands and he is on their side, Moses said. In fact, after we capture their land, Moses told them that when they kill some more animals to make a sacrifice, then all their sins will be erased and completely forgiven. So go get your promised land.

It appears that most slaves did not want war. They did not want to kill. They did not want to kidnap young virgin girls.

Remember that two major groups of verses have the whole story as Moses told it about why the trip was delayed for 40 years. They are Numbers 13 and 14.

In fact, if a query was made by a sensible adult in today's age of history, He/She would see no need to send a spy unit anywhere especially if God was actually travelling with your army of Terror. He (God) would just explain in detail what the land was like with each rock and each bend in the road and what he/she could do to equalize forces. If a God was actually with them, He would know their complete eight question answers about the land. This pretty well proves that NO GOD was with this terror army group.

The need to send spies and gather the answers to the 8 spy questions that were listed in the Bible might have fit old Biblical time men but the wool can't be pulled over the eyes of sensible, peace loving men in the 21st century. Men who want peace and not killing wars. They would just say, God if these people have sinned, punish them yourself.

Moses was just like Saddam Hussein who said God was on his side, so let's get the killings done and the new land captured, and the gold taken. What a disgrace to see millions of big time leaders not stand up for justice and peace! Just because religion is BIG, BIG, BIG time business. What do they think they are protecting? Many say it's their own tax deductions. What a shame. Is that possible?

There has been millions, both men and women before me to read this big Holy Bible book and all have shunned their responsibility of alerting the public as to exactly what is going on in this big terror plot to just take land that wasn't theirs to take. To kill, to torture men, their wives, their children and all their livestock in many instances, to just also take their fruit orchards in force.

Let us return to the story of Moses.

Moses remembers well many of his boy-hood days of being at the King's Palace. He was not allowed to play, fear of his own life. He was not allowed to go meet any arriving horse carriages also for fear of his life around any corner. Moses never did have a father to greet him and to wish him any kind of encouragements.

He remembers the King's Estate as being a really big place with lots of outbuildings. The King had horse handling buildings, feed storage buildings, meat smoke houses, a really big Servant quarters, crop producing equipment sheds, with fenced in animal fields, hog pens and sheep pens and lots to handle just about anything the King wanted done.

He had a big quarters and living space for about 115 concubines, their kitchens, baths, social rooms and individual bedrooms and dressing areas.

There was no electricity, just olive oil as lamp fuels. No running water. All the scrapes went to the hogs feeding.

He remembers close to his 5th birthday seeing several wagon loads of slaves show up at their place and started digging them two water wells. One for the King's Palace building and one for the Concubine living quarters. Before then, they had to haul water from the river daily for both places.

After the wells were dug, a bucket was lowered down into the wells to fetch and draw up water. It was sure clearer water than before using the river water especially after any rain storms.

Moses was not allowed to walk around any of the outbuildings except on days when the King was away from the Palace on business. He was forbidden to always stay away from over the valley near the Concubine quarters for fear of one of the female residence girls might see him and inquire to the King as to who the little boy was?

The King's Palace also had a large fruit orchard which was manned daily by half dozen men Servants way away from the main Palace building. Moses would have plenty of fruit given to him by his mother and some of the others which job was to keep Moses hid and raised out of trouble.

Moses had on occasions horse carriage trips to make through town and around the nearby country sides with his familiar trusted guardians to see and learn the whole area and what was being built and what was going on with others around all the lands. He would write and draw many pictures while he was out being shown the area like it was and would recopy it all much better when he returned home. He remembers being driven near by his relatives place several times. He saw Marian and Aaron at a distance on different occasions and was told who they were. The adults in the carriage told him that his mother Jachebed never had any other children. He stopped his carriage and talked to them on a couple occasions.

Moses loved to write and to keep Documents. Since his playing and socializing was very limited, He spent most all his spare time writing and making written scroll written records.

After his 12th year, he wanted to listen in on the King's weekly meetings more and learn knowledgeable techniques in the ways that decisions were made in settling disputes and being King in a powerful chair in charge of the land and people.

In the King's Palace, which was three story and big in size. He would hide himself in one of the upstairs balcony rooms on the third floor where the King very seldom went if ever. This balcony had a railing safety guard with long 12 feet hanging curtains which could be opened so the sitting people could watch the dance, play acting, roll playing, and other activities below on the main bottom downstairs floor. The balcony you could say, opened up to view the inside of the Palace instead of the outside. So the downstairs activities could be seen and heard.

The King could see from his downstairs, main floor throne all that was going on anytime he wanted to just look that direction. Sometimes, a group of practice sessions would start early in the morning for an evening play or demonstration of something. They would just repeat (practicing) over and over again any part of the play or activity they wanted to get more perfect all the long day. Practicing again and again.

Moses would stay upstairs in his portion of the third floor balcony and hear really good the King's meetings during the day and all the arguments and orders which were given by the King. Especially on those days when no practicing sessions were happening. He would hear all the proceedings really good. The King would always talk and order things in a loud voice. Moses could even see what was going by peeping out between the slit in the long curtains of his balcony anytime he wanted.

Moses' new mother finally moved her and her maidservants, maidens living quarters up to the third floor of the Palace so all could watch Moses at all times. The King had a balcony position room on the first floor where he went anytime at night when there was a play or dance to watch. There were nine balconies all together. Three on each floor. There was a large sitting and viewing room on the first floor next to the King's balcony.

Moses, over the years, made many excellent written notes of how to handle the individual proceedings during disputes of the court he listened to in the King's Palace.

He took the best and more meaningful written procedures on scrolls with him when he left the Palace the last time on foot, as he sat out to search for his new home. He buried these valuable scrolls on the mountain of God where he could always retrieve them for references. He took them with him on his last trip down the scared mountain on the long desert trip. Moses kept some good notes on what a person should do to be a good person. He just modified the King's sayings that he heard in meetings for several years over his long stay hearing stories in his growing up. He heard all kinds of disputes the people complained about while in the presence of the King. Moses modified these good rules to follow to be a better human being. They came in extremely handy when it was time to write what God must have wanted to have for a perfect society and Laws and Rules for the slave army. He added subjects to his notes and recordings weekly as time went by, trying to include all possible laws needed and animal sacrificing for the slave's army to follow. Just saying it had the blessings of their #1 invisible fellow traveler (God) in their huge caravan with them.

Once Moses started out with this big group of 12 different armies One in each area. It became extremely hard and difficult to continue spreading the sacrificed animals blood on so many rituals in the big, big tent. Killing so many animals daily was a big problem but it was all done by delegates and they all needed to eat, With no potatoes nor even any cucumbers like the slaves back in Egypt was accustomed too.

Moses kept up the public boastings that God was right there in the big tent all of Moses' slave trip thru the desert. Moses at no time ever told the slaves any really valuable information from God about how the wisdom had been increased. No plans of the future, No rapid eye movement info, no psychology laws nor rules to be a better one with their fellow human beings. Instead, Moses kept telling them of plagues to come, rock slinging procedures to be practiced daily, sword fighting improvements to be done to kill their own kin on occasions for practice. To keep in mind their promised land was waiting and it was full of milk and honey. Moses told all that the new promised land would be given to them. They were not told they would have to kill the present owners and then only after a war, they would get the land.

During the training days, the slaves taking all this war training was told it was for self defense only. But it was a big surprise to them when they saw the real light and purpose.

Anytime where God was supposed to have spoken to Moses, He could have easily slipped in words, a future term that would be used later in our civilization's existence but he never did. Proving that No God was ever present. There are hundreds of terms he could have used to give proof of his presence to future generations but none was seen. I would liked to have seen some terms like DNA, Nasa, Life expectancy improvements, Diseases Curtailed, and hundreds more but none were found.

70- See Exodus 40:2 Also 17.

¹And the LORD spake unto Moses, saying,

²On the first day of the first month shalt thou set up the tabernacle of the tent of the congregation.

There is an error in Moses' writing here in this above verse. It should state that it's the first day of the first month **in the second year.** Just like Exodus 40:17 does.

¹⁷And it came to pass in the first month **in the second year**, on the first day of the month, that the tabernacle was reared up.

It took the whole year of the first one, in the desert to build the tabernacle. The beginning of the 2nd year in the desert, it was raised and tested. It was a secret place for God to rest and travel with the terrorist army. No one but Moses could do the talking of what his Allah, God commanded him to say to the Israel army.

No one knows who Moses read the Instructions of God to. It says in Leviticus 9:5 all the congregation drew near and stood before the Lord below.

71- See Levitus 9:5 Contradiction, Not all over a million could gather.

⁵And they brought that which Moses commanded before the tabernacle of the congregation: and **all the congregation drew near and stood before the LORD.**

Let me remind the readers that we are talking about 12 armies (Each tribe has its own group) that was over 600,000 men. Even it's leaders would occupy a big space. Their wives and parents and grandparents would put the population over a million. It said, "All the congregation drew near". Without megaphones or loudspeakers, only a very few could ever hear and understand his words. Maybe 20 people nearby could hear clearly but not any of the others. Definitely not all the congregation like it says. Such devices for allowing others to hear AT A GATHERING did not exist then.

Moses treated his fellow slave people awful. He decided to go the long way around instead of the short nearest route to the promised land. Even in the beginning, Moses had decided that he had to work a plan or several plans to get rid of many stiff-necked people.

Here below are a few ways he slowly got rid of the whole adult clan. Instead of God being a loving and forgiving and teaching God, He chooses cruel punishment of Plagues and immediate death and was angry at the stiff-necked people almost daily, "burning with anger", it said.

72- See Numbers 5:15 thru 31. The Law of jealousy.

¹⁵**Then shall the man bring his wife unto the priest**, and he shall bring her offering for her, the tenth part of an ephah of barley meal; he shall pour no oil upon it, nor put frankincense thereon; **for it is an offering of jealousy**, an offering of memorial, bringing iniquity to remembrance.

¹⁶And the priest shall bring her near, and set her before the LORD:

¹⁷And the priest shall take holy water in an earthen vessel; **and of the dust that is in the floor of the tabernacle the priest shall take, and put it into the water:**

¹⁸And the priest shall set the woman before the LORD, and uncover the woman's head, and put the offering of memorial in her hands, **which is the jeal-**

ousy offering: and the priest shall have in his hand the bitter water that causeth the curse:

[19] And the priest shall charge her by an oath, and say unto the woman, if no man have lain with thee, and if thou hast not gone aside to uncleanness with another instead of thy husband, be thou free from this bitter water that causeth the curse:

[20] But if thou hast gone aside to another instead of thy husband, and if thou be defiled, and some man have lain with thee beside thine husband:

[21] Then the priest shall charge the woman with an oath of cursing, and the priest shall say unto the woman, The LORD make thee a curse and an oath among thy people, when the LORD doth make thy thigh to rot, and **thy belly to swell**;

[22] **And this water that causeth the curse shall go into thy bowels, to make thy belly to swell, and thy thigh to rot**: And the woman shall say, Amen, amen.

[23] And the priest shall write these curses in a book, and he shall blot them out with the bitter water:

[24] And he shall cause the woman to drink the bitter water that causeth the curse: and the water that causeth the curse shall enter into her, and become bitter.

²⁵Then the priest shall take the jealousy offering out of the woman's hand, and shall wave the offering before the LORD, and offer it upon the altar:

²⁶And the priest shall take an handful of the offering, even the memorial thereof, and burn it upon the altar, **and afterward shall cause the woman to drink the water.**

²⁷**And when he hath made her to drink the water, then it shall come to pass, that, if she be defiled, and have done trespass against her husband, that the water that causeth the curse shall enter into her, and become bitter, and her belly shall swell, and her thigh shall rot: and the woman shall be a curse among her people.**

²⁸And if the woman be not defiled, but be clean; then she shall be free, and shall conceive seed.

²⁹**This is the law of jealousies, when a wife goeth aside to another instead of her husband, and is defiled;**

³⁰Or when the spirit of jealousy cometh upon him, and he be jealous over his wife, and shall set the woman before the LORD, and **the priest shall execute upon her all this law.**

³¹**Then shall the man be guiltless from iniquity and this woman shall bear her iniquity.**

73- See Numbers 11:1 thru 35. Contradiction.

¹And when the people complained, it displeased the LORD: and the LORD heard it; and **his anger was kindled; and the fire of the LORD burnt among them, and consumed them that were in the uttermost parts of the camp.**

²And the people cried unto Moses; and when Moses prayed unto the LORD, the fire was quenched.

³And he called the name of the place Taberah: because the fire of the LORD burnt among them.

⁴**And the mix multitude that was among them fell a lusting: and the children of Israel also wept again, and said, who shall give us flesh to eat?**

⁵**We remember the fish, which we did eat in Egypt freely; the cucumbers, and the melons, and the leeks, and the onions, and the garlick:**

⁶**But now our soul is dried away: there is nothing at all, beside this manna, before our eyes.**

⁷And the manna was as coriander seed and the colour thereof as the colour of bdellium.

⁸And the people went about, and gathered it, and ground it in mills, or beat it in a mortar, and baked it in pans, and made cakes of it: and the taste of it was as the taste of fresh oil.

⁹**And when the dew fell upon the camp in the night, the manna fell upon it.**

¹⁰Then Moses heard the people weep throughout their families, every man in the door of his tent: and **the anger of the LORD was kindled greatly**; Moses also was displeased.

¹¹And Moses said unto the LORD, Wherefore hast thou afflicted thy servant? And wherefore have I not found favour in thy sight, that thou layest the burden of all this people upon me?

¹²Have I conceived all this people? Have I begotten them, that thou shouldest say unto me, Carry them in thy bosom, as a nursing father beareth the sucking child, unto the land which thou swarest unto their fathers?

¹³Whence should I have flesh to give unto all this people? For they weep unto me, saying, **Give us flesh, that we may eat.**

¹⁴I am not able to bear all this people alone, because it is too heavy for me.

¹⁵And if thou deal thus with me, kill me, I pray thee, out of hand, if I have found favour in thy sight; and let me not see my wretchedness.

¹⁶And the LORD said unto Moses, **Gather unto me seventy men of the elders of Israel, whom thou knowest to be the elders of the people, and offi-**

cers over them; and bring them unto the tabernacle of the congregation, that they may stand there with thee.

[17] And I will come down and talk with thee there: and I will take of the spirit which is upon thee, and will put it upon them; and they shall bear the burden of the people with thee, that thou bear it not thyself alone.

[18] And say thou unto the people, Sanctify yourselves against tomorrow, and ye shall eat flesh: for ye have wept in the ears of the LORD, saying, who shall give us flesh to eat? For it was well with us in Egypt: therefore the LORD will give you flesh and ye shall eat.

[19] **Ye shall not eat one day, nor two days, nor five days, neither ten days, nor twenty days;**

[20] **But even a whole month, until it come out at your nostrils, and it be loathsome unto you:** because that ye have despised the LORD which is among you, and have wept before him, saying, Why came we forth out of Egypt?

[21] And Moses said, **the people, among whom I am, are six hundred thousand footmen; and thou hast said, I will give them flesh, that they may eat a whole month.**

²²Shall the flocks and the herds be slain for them, to suffice them? Or shall all the fish of the sea be gathered together for them, to suffice them?

²³And the LORD said unto Moses, Is the LORD'S hand waxed short? Thou shalt see now whether my word shall come to pass unto thee or not.

²⁴And Moses went out, and told the people the words of the LORD, and **gathered the seventy men of the elders of the people, and set them round about the tabernacle.**

²⁵And the LORD came down in a cloud, and spake unto him, and took of the spirit that was upon him, **and gave it unto the seventy elders**: and it came to pass, that, when the spirit rested upon them, they prophesied, and did not cease.

²⁶But there remained two of the men in the camp, the name of the one was Eldad, and the name of the other Medad: and the spirit rested upon them; and they were of them that were written, but went not out unto the tabernacle: and they prophesied in the camp.

²⁷And there ran a young man, and told Moses, and said, Eldad and Medad do prophesy in the camp.

²⁸And Joshua the son of Nun, the servant of Moses, one of his young men, answered and said, my lord Moses, forbid them.

²⁹And Moses said unto him, Enviest thou for my sake? Would God that all the LORD'S people were prophets, and that the LORD would put his spirit upon them!

³⁰And Moses gat him into the camp, he and the elders of Israel.

³¹And there went forth a wind from the LORD, and **brought quails from the sea, and let them fall by the camp, as it were a day's journey on this side, and as it were a day's journey on the other side, round about the camp, and as it were two cubits high upon the face of the earth.**

³²**And the people stood up all that day, and all that night, and all the next day, and they gathered the quails:** he that gathered least gathered ten homers: and they spread them all abroad for themselves round about the camp.

³³**And while the flesh was yet between their teeth, ere it was chewed, the wrath of the LORD was kindled against the people, and the LORD smote the people with a very great plague.**

³⁴And he called the name of that place Kibrothhattaavah: **because there they buried the people that lusted.**

³⁵And the people journeyed from Kibrothhattaavah unto Hazeroth; and abode at Hazeroth.

Moses' meaning for the word "lusted" means those who are tired of the same old thing every day. Meat and Manna. They wished for something better like **fish, which we did eat in Egypt freely; the cucumbers, and the melons, and the leeks, and the onions, and the garlick:**

74- See Mathew 15:24 Jesus said he was sent to the people of Israel only. Contradiction

^{24}**But he answered and said, I am not sent but unto the lost sheep of the house of Israel.**

75- **See Judges 19:10 Jebus is the city of Jerusalem.**

^{10}But the man would not tarry that night, but he rose up and departed, **and came over against Jebus, which is Jerusalem**; and there were with him two asses saddled, his concubine also was with him.

76- Generations listing from God to Jesus. (76 Generations).

Father Son Notes
1- God Adam
2- Adam Seth 130 yrs
3- Seth Enosh 105 yrs
4- Enosh Kenan 89 yrs
5- Kenam Mahalalel 70 yrs
6- Mahalalel Jared 65 yrs
7- Jared Enoch 162 yrs
8- Enoch Metuselah Enoch walked w God. 65 yrs.
9- Methuselah Lamech 187 yrs
10- Lamech Noah 182 yrs
11- Noah Shem Noah, His wife, 3 Sons & wives 500 y
12- Shem Arphaxad 100 yrs
13- Arphaxad Cainan Cainan missing in Bible.
14- Cainan Shelah 35 yrs
15- Shelah Eber 30 yrs
16- Eber Peleg 34 yrs
17- Peleg Reu 30 yrs
18- Reu Serug 32 yrs

19- Serug Nahor 30 yrs
20- Nahor Terah 29 yrs
21- Terah Abraham 70 yrs
22- Abraham Isaac 100 yrs
23- Isaac Jacob ?
24- Jacob Judah Jacob worked for two wives.
25- Judah Perez ?
26- Perez Hezron
27- Hezron Ram
28- Ram Amminadab
29- Amminadab Nahshen
30- Nahshon Salmon
31- Salmon Boaz
32- Boaz Obed
33- Obed Jesse
34- Jesse David David became King.
35- David Natham David made Solomon King.
36- Natham Mattatha
37- Mattaha Menna
38- Menna Melea
39- Melea Eliakim
40- Eliakim Jonam
41- Jonam Joseph
42- Joseph Judah
43- Judah Simeon
44- Simeon Levi
45- Levi Matthat
46- Matthat Jorim
47- Jorim Eliezer
48- Eliezer Joshua
49- Joshua Er
50- Er Elmadam

51- Elmadam Cosam
52- Cosam Addi
53- Addi Melki
54- Melki Neri
55- Neri Shealtiel
56- Shealtiel Zerubbabel
57- Zerubbabel Rhesa
58- Rhesa Joanan
59- Joanan Joda
60- Joda Josech
61- Josech Semein
62- Semein Mattathias
63- Mattathias Maath
64- Maath Naggai
65- Naggai Esli
66- Elsi Nahum
67- Nahum Amos
68- Amos Mattathias
69- Mattathias Joseph
70- Joseph Jannai
71- Jannai Melki
72- Melki Levi
73- Levi Matthat
74- Matthat Heli
75- Heli Joseph
76- Joseph Jesus

I have shown the list of generations sequentially from God to Jesus. Bear in mind that it's not much usefulness because Joseph's DNA was not used in the chain because Mary was made expecting by the Holy Ghost.

Joseph's sperm was not used to create Jesus' DNA from any combined chromosomes from Joseph and Mary. Instead Mary's mixture of chromosomes for her baby Jesus was from God (Holy Ghost) and Mary.

77- See Mathew 1:18 and also 23.

[18] Now the birth of Jesus Christ was on this wise: When as his mother Mary was espoused to Joseph, before they came together, she was found with child of the Holy Ghost.

[23] Behold, a virgin shall be with child, and shall bring forth a son, and they shall call his name Emmanuel, which being interpreted is, God with us.

A BIBLICAL EGYPTIAN SLAVE'S KNOWLEDGE

This author worked many long hours during many early before twilight to dawn hours putting down on paper what a longtime old Biblical era Egyptian told me to write about. It's a long part of Moses period of history. I had great success in the readings of Bridie Murphy story in 1955, doing research. Edgar Cacye story in 1965 doing more research. The Oahspe Bible in 1975 adding more research. Now, I am writing this story in this new book what I have researched.

> My name is Gershom. I am the tenth son to Nadabi. He was my father parent while crossing the Desert for 30 years. He tells me that he was busy crossing the Desert for 10 years before I was born. He had bad health and joined his fathers who were sleeping when he was 66 years old. I enjoyed my 30 years with him. He taught me and all my brothers 20 of them how to fight for his land that had been promised to be given to him. They would have to fight and kill many first to get this Promised Land. What

a terrible deal, I wish my parents had stayed in Egypt. My father and Mother told me all about this fella Moses and how he was before he died. My Dad gave on to me all his diary notes he had been taking before his bad health took over and not allowed him to write anymore.

I could use the rock sling pretty accurately and with good precision as Moses' leaders trained me daily except on Sundays. I could hit a cactus bush anywhere anyone else told me that they want it hit. I couldn't for a few years when I started but I finally perfected it. I was really great!

This is another part of the Moses story which has never been told. Remember that over one million slaves counting the members of each slave family was on the move to another country. We do not know exactly anything positive about all of them except that Moses and also God proclaimed that we were stupid people. Stubborn, they said. Every few days that passed, God wanted to kill many of us. Kill his own creations and Moses and God did just that.

As Professor Roy Yonce has ask me to explain, A slaves duties, an outlook on happenings, people and conditions as I saw them. I will assume to be just one of the average slave members for a moment and try to pretend just what one slave would have said. My name is Gershom. I am with a huge, great big group that is on the move. We have many unknowns ahead. Many of us have to drive the animals and livestock along the trail and we don't even know where we will find water or grass for any animals for them to eat and drink along the way. We don't even know where we are going.

Many of my friends I know can't read, nor write as they have been a slave all their lives. My mother and father before me were slaves. Their parents were slaves. And also were my great grandparents, slaves that were not taught much except to rise at dawn, eat breakfast and work all day. We got pretty much plenty to eat but we had a huge fatality rate. Probably due to cruelty to slaves and no medicines except some special selected herbs that helped sometimes our condition. We ate the same diet day in and day out. Nothing changed. The water was dirty many times. We would change the water containers with fresher water whenever we would come to a creek, river, or town that would allow us to replenish supplies. I can remember many times standing knee high in a creek bed and while other bathed, all around me, I would be refilling my drinking water utensils and all containers with hopefully better water than I had before. We did not know how to value water except it would pour out and leave mud in the bottom.

I did not know any big words to speak except "get the hay in", "feed the animals", and "old curry has died". I suppose the very largest word I could say was magician. I had heard about them, they were magic Gods the type that could do all sorts of things that amazed everyone, and kept one spellbound with his/her powers. God was the leader over all

Magicians in our camp. Moses knew the most about how to do it at the right times.

Moses was 120 years old when we walked into Moab. Moses died when he went up the mountain, called Nebo. I was one of the army's fighting team when we were sent up to take over the territory of Geshur but we could not drive out those people. We also could not drive out the people from Mascah. We also could not drive out the people from Jebus and many other lands. One reason is they had fast moving chariots that we could not run fast enough to keep up and catch them. They were also very good and accurate at spear throwing.

Joshua died when he was 110 years old. I saw him giving talks before he died. Neither Moses nor Joshua were ever good at giving speeches. They seemed to forget what they were talking about a lot. My close friends and some relatives were able to choose our representative, the one we sent along with the group of 13 other men, to check out the land called Eshcol, A morites, Kadesh Barnea, to find out what kind of fight We would have to make to take over our promised land. It was awful there. Giants, highwalls, we looked like grasshoppers compared to them. Nobody thought we could corner them and take our promised lands. Just so many big, big, strong males that could break your arm or leg with their bare hands. They seemed to be trained in other war fare than we were. Most all the men from our teams become frightened just being around them. God really got mad about something we said and we were made more scared when we found out he wasn't going to help us. Then we heard that God gave up on us and said that all of us adults would die in the desert and not see the land he promised us. God must understand that we are not fools and would not jump into a fight when we saw no way of winning.

At times, we slaves said between ourselves that this God who was always in the big tent sleeping did nothing magic to help in our jobs and what Moses wanted us to do daily. If we just had a smarter God with us, then not 14 spies would be needed to be sent to check out this land in the first place. If some returned with not enough confidence to take the land in a fight, then not 14 spies would have been able to change a smart loving God from his/her plans and cause them to change our trip to get this land over 40 years later after all the adults in our army had died off. It's such a sad occurrence to see the Moses story go down the drain without more clever analyzations done by more experienced men with research to examine his scrolls materials much closer. After Moses died, my relatives got hold of Moses' scrolls and they all had many things that were not so written in them. Moses just right out lied about many things. There must be willing people somewhere willing to finally expose the many contradictions. There are just so many statements that just does not make good senses to future generations that want the truth instead of a materials washing scheme. My mind at the time of living as a slave in Moses' army was very limited as I had no education except war fare techniques to acquire real estate. But now after reincarnated memories of jogging the recall, I can interpret my past knowledge from my past Hebrew language to Professor Roy Yonce's present English language really well and accurate. In this mind of after translating has been accomplished, I have so much more available in my viewing mind. Somehow, translating my past viewed memory causes so much more reasoning explanations during translation periods than my mind knew at the time with no education. It's amazing and I can't explain how the mind is working to achieve this.

When my folks examined Moses' scrolls, God's supremacy and dogmatic power was shown all throughout. Yet he said many things that wasn't so. God's none loving attitude was pointed out and painted all over his scrolls. His absence of human beings heart knowledge was clearly exposed. Moses did all the God's speaking for him. Moses clearly had his own biases in all of God's words. It's the very first terrorist printed story ever published. Hatred, Greed, Sins, Murders, Robbery, Killings, Kidnappings and more evil dominated the whole set of 35 long scrolls.

I can remember my parents telling me about their first meetings and first knowledge they knew of this man Moses. We did not know anything about this fellow named Moses when he came to town they said, except he had bigger magic than the Pharaoh's magicians. We heard that he showed Pharaoh several magic tricks. They then had a contest and the winner of those tricks was to be the ones to get control of all us slaves.

Well what a group of days those were, Moses and his brother Aaron, did their tricks and Pharaoh's magicians matched it. Then another and another and Pharaoh's master men matched every one of them and performed the same thing they did. Then when Moses did not allow Pharaoh's magic men enough time to prepare and even practice, Moses won because Pharaoh's men needed more time. It always takes time to practice all magic tricks to do them good. Moses began to win more and more and Pharaoh got really sick. One particular trick, Moses team said they were going to kill the very first born male animals of all groups and also the very first born male of each family that Pharaoh had. Wow! It worked and he won. He did it with great magic and without laying a hand on anybody. Pharaoh did not want to try that one. No Sir Ree! Pharaoh told his magicians to just let Moses and his team have all of the slaves as soon as he could get them going out of town.

My parents said they left Egypt right away. They made it all the way into the desert while Pharaoh was burying their dead. My parents said they do not know where they were going. They had to listen to that fellow Moses constantly saying, "Get those livestock moving faster, we can't stop here". We had all kinds of animals wanting to stop and eat what they saw and take their time. Moses was a pusher and was always saying "Hurry it up!", "Let's get going further along". All day long he was saying it. We ended up killing at least half dozen of these male animals for all kinds of Sacrifices, even grain offerings daily with another half dozen as meat to feed the big over a million crew along the trip. Some we had to kill in the early mornings and others after the sun went down daily. We also had Sin offering Sacrifices which erase or cancel each and every sin any of us did that day. Now that was really great magic for all of us. Amazing beyond belief. We could even murder and it be forgiven with a little bit of sweet smelling smoke pleasing to all of us.

I remember one particular time when Moses ask for each of us to pay and come up with a tax of some sort of offering saying it was for the price of each of us. We were somehow paying him for having our freedom back and not being owned as a slave anymore. He says we were actually paying for our lives. I still do not understand that. I, nor any of my parents, grandparents have never been free before. We have always been slaves.

I ask my parents and they don't know either. Why didn't Moses use some of his magic for us to get or acquire some of those 600 chariots and horses that my parents told me got drowned of Pharaoh's army. We had to carry all this baggage load of stuff on our shoulders for days and it turned into years and years as we were always moving across the desert. I guess that I was a dumb stubborn slave and was not supposed to know why. Just work my ass off every day, and carry that load.

But I still resent that and many other foolish things. I resent most a none-loving God, a cruel slave driver as both Moses and God proved to all of us to be. They led us on a wild goose chase way out of the way instead of direct to that prize honey and milk Promised Land. It has turned into hate after awhile with all the false promises.

We all came to this big mountain my parents said, along the trail that he said he was going up to the top of it and talk to God about the work he was supposed to get done of carrying this huge caravan of people, livestock and supplies across this sandy desert. He said he did not know the way to this Promised Land or how we could get to it but said he was going to spend several weeks up on top of this mountain talking to God. Then he would come back down the mountain and tell us slaves all his conversations he had with his God. He said to my parents that he had been up on top of this mountain before and saw God and talked with him only a few months ago.

Well, the surprising thing is that he was extremely strict about him going up this mountain all by himself. He told all of us that if anybody tried to follow him up that mountain that they would be killed, he specifically said to stone anyone to death that tried to follow, or shoot them with arrows from a bow. My great buddy Harry was killed along with many others. Thank goodness, I did not try to see what God looked like and how he taught Moses all those tricks. We all wanted to watch Moses with his magic for so many weeks. I know he took his hammer and rock chisel with him. My parents stayed down at the bottom they said because so many others got killed.

Well when this fellow Moses finally came back down the mountain, after 40 days, he could not be reasoned with said my parents. We knew enough even slaves, to know that a real God, one that has real love and was proud of his/her creations, would not need any human to walk/climb up any mountain to talk with him. If He was a real, true, loving God, he could talk to any of his creations anywhere they were, in a tent, in a cave; it did not need a trip a top of any mountain. He threw down all he was carrying along with him. It made him so mad to see all the engineering that had been done without his help. He wanted to control it all. My parents ask him what on earth had he been eating daily while up on top of that mountain? He said fruit, berries, and honey, but he missed his meat.

He took that golden calf my parents friends had made and he broke it all apart. He burned it and melted it and put the liquid remains in a drink and made all the ones that had anything to do with suggesting it to be made to drink that melted golden calf. (All but his brother Aaron, He did not make him drink that terrible colored awful tasting drink). Well, it was a good thing he didn't drink any because all the others that did drink any, died. They blamed it on a Plague of some sort. I am smart enough to know that if one drinks any rusty looking water then he will clog up his pipes and kidneys fail big time.

Like its dying time after just a few drinks. I am so glad my parents did not drink any. My parents' good buddy Jacob and his relatives just keeled over and died right on the spot. My parents had to haul off over 2,000 of their bodies to the woods and leave them after undressing their bodies and saving their clothes. Moses said wild beast needed their bodies as food.

Let me tell you something about that fellow Moses before I forget it. My parents said that Moses was raised in Pharaoh's Palace. One of Pharaoh's daughters raised him. She kept him pretty well hid from her father for many years as her father really hated all Hebrew male children.

In Moses boyhood days, The King was always hollering and giving orders and demands that was not fit for a good human to even hear. One Moses heard very clear was to select 600 pretty, virgins from families and to take them from their house by the King's orders . Give them to his army commanders on a yearly basis as well as other orders to cruel to even talk about.

It was after our first resting stop was over on the west side of the red sea; we had past the red sea. We had travelled about three days none stop and had reached the 2nd major rest spot. As we were getting our breath and energy recharged. This fellow Moses said to our leaders about increasing our army size. My parents told me all about it. He told the group leaders while they were together saying now while we were in the clear of any enemies like Pharaoh's army that we had to put our baby manufacturers (the women) to work in producing more off-springs to help us on the long trip. Well the leaders couldn't get out of their meeting soon enough to spread the good news. They told all about how we must spend several days right there in that resting spot on the desert to get busy pro-creating more of an army than we had so far. They told my parents and others that we would be needing much more help to get where we were going. We had to get the baby manufacturing rolling big time and in overtime. After a few months, we had dozens being born in our camp daily. I can remember my parents saying that about 9 months later after the first talk about producing babies that they had 568 new babies born in just one day throughout the camp. It was a high number every day from then on. Those that had a wife really liked the idea and all those men which were not married to a pretty female found one the very same day when the pro-creation plan was sanctioned and announced by the leaders.

Not all days were filled with pleasure nor even happy ones though, because Moses or either God was always threatening us to get killed. God did kill thousands every few days as he carried out his none loving, not caring plans. He appeared to be an extremely mean magician always showing his hot burning temper and burning anger. He would even get mad at us slaves even suggesting anything at all, at anytime. We were just not allowed to develop into leaders. Only Moses wanted to be a leader. I guess because only he knew all the magic. In my later years, it was told to me by Moses, that God could make anybody sad, happy, wise, or learned but I can't remember ever knowing that God ever made any of us slaves really happy nor smart. He would just poured out his anger on us at the least little suggestion we made. Then I would lose many more of my close friends and relatives by just watching them get a plague and die. Sometimes, God would even kill the entire family members. Babies included. He showed all of us that he didn't care for his own supposed to be personal creations.

I was not born at that time yet but after I was a little boy and they told me about it, I knew right then and there that Moses so called God and his very strange behavior of not letting even his own sister Marian talk to God that his made up story of God was fishy and could not be real and even trusted.

I added up hundreds of supposed to have happened incidents that did not make good sense when I saw his many scrolls he had written. Many of the other slaves thought the same as I. We were still slaves like before, just with a new owner and much less to eat and drink with much more walking.

Another major error on Moses part was not allowing God to kill his own enemies himself. He was much more equipped to dish out due punishment himself. Like that poor old man who was stoned to death for picking up sticks on Sunday. All those hundreds of others Moses has had us to stone to death because he wanted revenge himself. It just proves to me that this God figure was in Moses head and not for real in the tent. Moses worked for a whole year my parents said building the huge big oversized tent for the supposed home of God. The scrolls says otherwise as some sort of psychology written to Joshua as help in suggestions to continue the fabrication.

Remember that Moses gave the order also that absolutely anyone approaching that tent at the wrong time must be put to death. He also said that earlier according to my parents that anyone approaching even the foot of the mountain would be put to death.

In Moses scrolls about the big tent, He was able to spend a whole year building it just to proclaim and help to prove to us slaves that he really had God chained to a bed in that tent where god slept day and night helping his army with lots of magic. But killing all he could to get even every week he could.

You just didn't see nor talk to God at anytime. EVER! Unless your name was Moses. After Moses died, the same pretending continued on Joshua's watch.

My slave contact, in the very early morning hours, Gershom also told me about his many friends and relatives who were also killed by God when they expressed a desire to have something else to eat besides of the simple diet they were being fed daily.

He said his parents remembered eating cucumbers, melons, onions, garlic and other things to eat all the time back in Egypt. But for many days, all they have had in the desert all they have seen is that Manna. They thought it was a great idea to balance their intake diet like they once did back in Egypt. But God and Moses got really hot burning with anger at the very first mention of this added balanced food diet idea.

Gershom continues to tell us about this present God they had. He cannot read their thoughts and minds like a real, true, loving God can. God only got mad after some representatives announced to Moses days later that the groups had been secretly wishing, praying, and thinking about so much better of a balanced diet like they once had back in Egypt. That's when this so called God got so angry that he killed all those who wished for a better balanced diet. Gershom said it was caused somehow by Moses magic because their God did absolutely nothing for weeks about it until the very day these representatives spoke and expressed their desires to Moses. A very strange occurrence indeed! Their God knew nothing about their prayers and wishful thinking for weeks. It was only after they had told Moses the people were unhappy of their diet. Gershom says there were just so many hundreds of things that Moses and his supposed to be God did that doesn't seem to add up to be any kind of normal expected occurrence.

Gershom continues to say, the army of Moses could have slaves, servants both men and women, menservants and women servants, Also concubines. They could also have multiple wives. There were set prices to pay the priest, for each classification, one had to pay for that life. Also to give animals as Sin offerings to the Priest to be forgiven all sins which were completely exonerated and forgiven.

It was an important part of being a part of the distributed plunder booty gathered so one could afford more of the kidnapped persons one needed back in the army camp.

The virgin females were allowed to mate and become promised to a man at their reached birthday of 14. They had coming of age parties in each group. The females had to be married to men only in their representative groups. This was Moses' explanation of demanding that all property rights stay with a chosen family or a chosen group of their father's name could not be transferred between different army groups. Any single females had to marry within their own army group. A male could speak for any female he wanted in his own group at the coming of age party which were held monthly in the entire camp, and her fee paid to the priest.

78- See Numbers 14:22 thru 39. Contradiction

^{22}Because all those men which have seen my glory, and my miracles, which I did in Egypt and in the wilderness, **and have tempted me now these ten times, and have not hearkened to my voice;**

²³Surely they shall **not see** the land which I sware unto their fathers, neither **shall any of them that provoked me see it:**

²⁴But my servant Caleb, because he had another spirit with him, and hath followed me fully, him will I bring into the land whereinto he went; and his seed shall possess it.

²⁵(Now the Amalekites and the Canaanites dwelt in the valley.) Tomorrow turn you, and get you into the wilderness by the way of the Red sea.

²⁶And the LORD spake unto Moses and unto Aaron, saying,

²⁷How **long shall I bear with this evil congregation, which murmur against me? I have heard the murmurings of the children of Israel, which they murmur against me.**

²⁸Say unto them, as truly as I live, saith the LORD, as ye have spoken in mine ears, so will I do to you:

²⁹**Your carcasses shall fall in this wilderness; and all that were numbered of you, according to your whole number, from twenty years old and upward which have murmured against me.**

³⁰Doubtless ye shall **not come into the land**, concerning which I sware to make you dwell therein, save Caleb the son of Jephunneh, and Joshua the son of Nun.

³¹But your little ones, which ye said should be a prey, them will I bring in, and **they shall know the land which ye have despised.**

³²**But as for you, your carcasses, they shall fall in this wilderness.**

³³**And your children shall wander in the wilderness forty years, and bear your whoredoms, until your carcasses be wasted in the wilderness.**

³⁴After the number of the days in which ye searched the land, **even forty days, each day for a year, shall ye bear your iniquities, even forty years, and ye shall know my breach of promise.**

³⁵I the LORD have said, **I will surely do it unto all this evil congregation, that are gathered together against me: in this wilderness they shall be consumed, and there they shall die.**

³⁶And the men, which Moses sent to search the land, who returned, and made all the congregation to murmur against him, by bringing up a slander upon the land,

³⁷**Even those men that did bring up the evil report upon the land, died by the plague before the LORD.**

³⁸**But Joshua the son of Nun, and Caleb the son of Jephunneh, which were of the men that went to search the land, lived still.**

³⁹**And Moses told these sayings unto all the children of Israel: and the people mourned greatly.**

What a mean and cruel way to act for a God. He falls short or keeping his previous sworn statement of even letting people dwell in the Promised Land. I think this is just more proof of how insensitive and cruel this God was that didn't care about his created people. It's just more evidence that Moses made it all up. He wanted to prove that God was with him and with his killing ideas! Notice from the beginning, Moses or the writer tries to convince all readers that his God is right along with him giving the Israel army new inhabitants status of the promise land.

It just adds up to more Moses' wishes to have his trained Terror Army to kill, kill and steal and take this Promised Land as he promised it himself. No actual real live God ever promised it. "Thou shalt not kill" commandment was just set aside long enough to get the job done! Take the land, livestock, virgins, and fruit by force!

Looks like he has gotten away with it for many thousands of years. Many of those who saw the Dictator story, the real facts unfold, tuned into AETHEIST.

No I will never be an Atheist. I believe in the compound elements, and so many other facts that I have uncovered in my 77 years of living. Yes, there is a God and his work is done through Psychics and others that dream of the hereafter for their little ones.

Read my over 200 pages, full color Auto-Biography book for a better understanding of my concepts, already printed and published.

An Active Life time Researcher, Thank you, Professor Roy Yonce

MODERN, PC APPLICATION PROGRAM CALLED BIBLE CODES

As readers of the very latest information on the authorized King James version Bible. Let me add an introduction that many of you are studying this subject will want to know about if you haven't gotten wind of it already. It's my extra bonus materials. Its introduction is placed within my manual. I do not sell them but recommend them.

In the 1980's a certain personal computer (PC) Software came about where it checks for hidden messages in the Hebrew version of the Holy Bible. Presto! It found many, amazing messages. These hidden messages were like a crossword puzzle once shown and printed out. Words meaningful to the Search Title showed themselves all around it in Vertical displacements, Horizontal displacements, backwards displacements, diagonally displacements.

These displacement words secretly was found by searching every 2nd, 3rd and so forth letter in the sequential Hebrew Bible. In the Hebrew Bible, there are no spaces used between words like our English language uses. Say as an example, every 944th letter spelled out a perfectly coherent word which had a major roll or relative to the Title search.

It was an amazing discovery! It gave one a new meaning entirely to the usage of the King James Holy Bible. It was a marvelous break through! I bought me one of those very first Software programs which searched the Hebrew Bible entirely and found many, many searched titles and their corresponding displacements of cross word like printed in readable details. One does not have to know Hebrew, but it would be a fantastic advantage. It also searches the King James English version. Say as an example, I used John F Kennedy as my title search. Then run the program, it would then search the whole Bible and find any words that made sense at every numerical position. Called and referred to as Equal-Distance searches. (**ELS codes**) The results came back with things like "Grassy Knoll", "Lee Harvey Oswell", "Killed in Dallas", and others.

I have used that program to search hundreds of Title search words or sentences. The program would come back with many, many meaningful displacements, words that related to its title.

I do believe that most every person who has ever been important came back with great results. Like one more example. Thomas Edison. Came back with

"Light Bulb", and other meaningful displaced words of inventions done by him.

I later recently in the year end of 2008, bought the next advanced Software program version release which runs on your best IBM compatible PC. It was fantastic! I use it all the time. Here is there www address if you are interested in getting this Software program. New Release: 20th September 2008

Code Finder: Millennium Edition, by Research Systems, (Win 95 to XP) as of 2009.

1. **Code Finder: Millenium Edition:** Search up to 500 individual terms at once, at a blinding speed, faster than all others. In using Code Finder: ME, the program designates the first term in the search list as the main/key term and matches all other terms to it based on the desired size matrix set in Settings. As a plus, Code Finder: ME is also the only program that allows toroidal searches (circular text). All other programs allow a straight codes search as if the text were a straight line with no spaces between the letters. Code Finder: ME allows a straight search text and also a toroidal search where the beginning and end of the search text are connected (a circular text). Many of the incredible matrixes I've done lately have been toroidal matrixes (for example, the matrixes shown on the last two History Channel specials: End of Days matrix and WMD from Iraq matrix). Superior automatic terms matching. http://www.codefinder.us/

Today we are pleased to announce the availability of the very latest in Bible Code Software with the public release of Code Finder Millennium Edition version 1.23. This release has more features than ever before and comes complete with totally reworked and expanded tutorial and online help information. This digitally signed software package is 100% compatible with all Windows versions from 98 through to Vista. With more features and no increase in price Code Finder now is greater value than ever before. Six years in development, version 1.23 incorporates requests from Code Finder users around the globe that greatly enhance this release. Download today and be searching for your own Bible Codes in minutes with the very latest in Bible Code technology.

Code Finder Millennium Edition on TV. Code Finder is frequently shown in action on the History Channel TV documentaries *The Bible Code: Predicting Armageddon* and *Bible Code II: Apocalypse and Beyond*.

> It means that any of these corresponding cross word like phases had to be put into the Bible 2000 years ago when it was written. That's extremely sophisticated to show up now in our age of the Desk Top PC.
>
> Even Twin Towers will come back with exactly meaningful corresponding information.
>
> I have done my own name and each of my immediate family member's names and friends. I have done everything I could think to search. It's an ex-

tremely valuable piece of PC Software for me to use 24/7 when I want to search for anything on my own PC.

It's called "Bible Codes" **Code Finder Millennium Edition is the very best as of this book's printing.**

Good Luck, Thank you, Professor Roy Yonce...

79- See Numbers 33:1 thru 49

¹**These are the journeys of the children of Israel, which went forth out of the land of Egypt with their armies under the hand of Moses and Aaron.**

²And Moses wrote their goings out according to their journeys by the commandment of the LORD: and **these are their journeys according to their goings out.**

³**And they departed from Rameses in the first month, on the fifteenth day of the first month;** on the morrow after the Passover **the children of Israel went out with an high hand in the sight of all the Egyptians.**

⁴For the Egyptians buried all their firstborn, which the LORD had smitten among them: upon their gods also the LORD executed judgments.

⁵And the children of Israel removed from Rameses, and pitched in Succoth.

⁶And they departed from Succoth, and pitched in Etham, which is in the edge of the wilderness.

⁷And they removed from Etham, and turned again unto Pihahiroth, which is before Baalzephon: and they pitched before Migdol.

⁸And they departed from before Pihahiroth, and passed through the midst of the sea into the wilderness, and went three days 'journey in the wilderness of Etham, and pitched in Marah.

⁹And they removed from Marah, and came unto Elim: and in Elim were twelve fountains of water, and threescore and ten palm trees; and they pitched there.

¹⁰And they removed from Elim, and encamped by the Red sea.

¹¹And they removed from the Red sea, and encamped in the wilderness of Sin.

¹²And they took their journey out of the wilderness of Sin, and encamped in Dophkah.

¹³And they departed from Dophkah, and encamped in Alush.

¹⁴And they removed from Alush, and encamped at Rephidim, where was no water for the people to drink.

¹⁵And they departed from Rephidim, and pitched in the wilderness of Sinai.

¹⁶And they removed from the desert of Sinai, and pitched at Kibrothhattaavah.

¹⁷And they departed from Kibrothhattaavah, and encamped at Hazeroth.

¹⁸And they departed from Hazeroth, and pitched in Rithmah.

¹⁹And they departed from Rithmah, and pitched at Rimmonparez.

²⁰And they departed from Rimmonparez, and pitched in Libnah.

²¹And they removed from Libnah, and pitched at Rissah.

²²And they journeyed from Rissah, and pitched in Kehelathah.

²³And they went from Kehelathah, and pitched in mount Shapher.

²⁴And they removed from mount Shapher, and encamped in Haradah.

²⁵And they removed from Haradah, and pitched in Makheloth.

²⁶ And they removed from Makheloth, and encamped at Tahath.

²⁷ And they departed from Tahath, and pitched at Tarah.

²⁸ And they removed from Tarah, and pitched in Mithcah.

²⁹ And they went from Mithcah, and pitched in Hashmonah.

³⁰ And they departed from Hashmonah, and encamped at Moseroth.

³¹ And they departed from Moseroth, and pitched in Benejaakan.

³² And they removed from Benejaakan, and encamped at Horhagidgad.

³³ And they went from Horhagidgad, and pitched in Jotbathah.

³⁴ And they removed from Jotbathah, and encamped at Ebronah.

³⁵ And they departed from Ebronah, and encamped at Eziongaber.

³⁶ And they removed from Eziongaber, and pitched in the wilderness of Zin, which is Kadesh.

³⁷And they removed from Kadesh, and pitched in mount Hor, in the edge of the land of Edom.

³⁸And Aaron the priest went up into mount Hor at the commandment of the LORD, and died there, in the fortieth year after the children of Israel were come out of the land of Egypt, in the first day of the fifth month.

³⁹And **Aaron was an hundred and twenty and three years old when he died in mount Hor.**

⁴⁰And king Arad the Canaanite, which dwelt in the south in the land of Canaan, heard of the coming of the children of Israel.

⁴¹And they departed from mount Hor, and pitched in Zalmonah.

⁴²And they departed from Zalmonah, and pitched in Punon.

⁴³And they departed from Punon, and pitched in Oboth.

⁴⁴And they departed from Oboth, and pitched in Ijeabarim, in the border of Moab.

⁴⁵And they departed from Iim, and pitched in Dibongad.

⁴⁶And they removed from Dibongad, and encamped in Almondiblathaim.

⁴⁷ And they removed from Almondiblathaim, and pitched in the mountains of Abarim, before Nebo.

⁴⁸ And they departed from the mountains of Abarim, and pitched in the plains of Moab by Jordan near Jericho.

⁴⁹ And they pitched by Jordan, from Bethjesimoth even unto Abelshittim in the plains of Moab.

⁵⁰ And the LORD spake unto Moses in the plains of Moab by Jordan near Jericho, saying,

⁵¹ Speak unto the children of Israel, and say unto them, When ye are passed over Jordan into the land of Canaan;

⁵² Then ye shall drive out all the inhabitants of the land from before you, and destroy all their pictures, and destroy all their molten images, and quite pluck down all their high places:

⁵³ And ye shall dispossess the inhabitants of the land, and dwell therein: for I have given you the land to possess it.

⁵⁴ And ye shall divide the land by lot for an inheritance among your families: and to the more ye shall give the more inheritance, and to the fewer ye shall give the less inheritance: every man's inheritance shall be in the place where his lot falleth; according to the tribes of your fathers ye shall inherit.

⁵⁵But if ye will not drive out the inhabitants of the land from before you; then it shall come to pass, that those which ye let remain of them shall be pricks in your eyes, and thorns in your sides, and shall vex you in the land wherein ye dwell.

⁵⁶Moreover it shall come to pass, that I shall do unto you, as I thought to do unto them.

> Above are 62 different places of stay, The Israel's slave army stopped at for awhile during their 40 years.

Picture taken of Professor Roy Yonce in about 2004. He wrote this book during 2009. It took many hours' research for Eight months dedicated, reading and note taking of the facts to expose the results.

80- See Deuteronomy 5:25 Contradiction

²⁵Now therefore why should we die? For this great fire will consume us: if we hear the voice of the LORD our God any more, then we shall die.

81- See Matthew 17:1 thru 13

¹And **after six days Jesus taketh Peter, James, and John his brother, and bringeth them up into an high mountain apart,**

²And **was transfigured before them: and his face did shine as the sun, and his raiment was white as the light.**

³And, **behold, there appeared unto them Moses and Elias talking with him.**

⁴Then answered Peter, and said unto Jesus, Lord, it is good for us to be here: if thou wilt, let us make here three tabernacles; one for thee, and one for Moses, and one for Elias.

⁵While he yet spake, behold, a bright cloud overshadowed them: and behold a voice out of the cloud, which said, this is my beloved Son, in whom I am well pleased; hear ye him.

⁶And when the disciples heard it, they fell on their face, and were sore afraid.

⁷And Jesus came and touched them, and said, Arise, and be not afraid.

⁸And when they had lifted up their eyes, they saw no man, save Jesus only.

⁹And as they came down from the mountain, Jesus charged them, saying, Tell the vision to no man, until the Son of man be risen again from the dead.

¹⁰And his disciples asked him, saying, why then say the scribes **that Elias must first come?**

¹¹And Jesus answered and said unto them, **Elias truly shall first come, and restore all things.**

¹²But I say unto you, That Elias is come already, and they knew him not, but have done unto him whatsoever they listed. Likewise shall also the Son of man suffer of them.

¹³Then **the disciples understood that he spake unto them of John the Baptist.**

It appears that John the Baptist was reincarnated from a previous Spirit of Elijah.

That is why Jesus called up two previous dead spirits.

Moses and Elias were called to awaken and speak to Jesus.

This was more info telling people about Reincarnation but the King's publishing people censored the Bible's published materials on several subjects. Reincarnation was one held back.

82- See Judges 20:15 thru 17

¹⁵And the children of Benjamin **were numbered at that time out of the cities twenty and six thousand men that drew sword, beside the inhabitants of Gibeah, which were numbered seven hundred chosen men.**

¹⁶**Among all this people there were seven hundred chosen men left-handed; every one could sling stones at an hair breadth, and not miss.**

¹⁷And **the men of Israel, beside Benjamin, were numbered four hundred thousand men that drew sword: all these were men of war.**

Verse 16 above were marksmen of such good quality that they could sling a rock and never miss hitting a hair.

83- See Judges 20:23 Contradiction

²³(And the children of Israel went up and wept before the LORD until even, and asked counsel of the LORD, saying, Shall I go up again to battle against the children of Benjamin my brother? And the LORD said, Go up against him.)

²⁴And the children of Israel came near against the children of Benjamin the second day.

²⁵And **Benjamin** went forth against them out of Gibeah the second day, and destroyed down to the ground of the children of Israel again eighteen thousand men; all these drew the sword.

Brother against Brother and one army killed 18,000 with swords. What a sad ending for two brothers to fight and wipe out the other.

84- See John 21:19 thru 24.

¹⁹This spake he, signifying by what death he should glorify God. And when he had spoken this, he saith unto him, follow me.

²⁰Then Peter, turning about, seeth the disciple whom Jesus loved following; which also leaned on his breast at supper, and said, Lord, which is he that betrayeth thee?

²¹Peter seeing him saith to Jesus, Lord, and what shall this man do?

²²Jesus saith unto him, If I will that he tarry till I come, what is that to thee? Follow thou me.

²³Then went this saying abroad among the brethren, that that disciple should not die: yet Jesus said not unto him, He shall not die; but, If I will that he tarry till I come, what is that to thee?

[24] This is the disciple which testifieth of these things, and wrote these things: and we know that his testimony is true.

> Jesus lets one particular disciple live and not die until he returns at his second coming.

> The Dead Sea scrolls state he allowed three disciples to remain living and not die. One was his servant wife, Mary.

> This is one reason the very first person Jesus visited after raising from the dead was Mary. He loved her most.

85- See John 19:25 thru 42. Three Marys at Jesus' death.

[25] Now there stood by the cross of Jesus his mother, and his mother's sister, Mary the wife of Cleophas, and Mary Magdalene.

[26] When Jesus therefore saw his mother, and the disciple standing by, whom he loved, he saith unto his mother, Woman, behold thy son!

[27] Then saith he to the disciple, Behold thy mother! And from that hour that disciple took her unto his own home.

²⁸After this, Jesus knowing that all things were now accomplished, that the scripture might be fulfilled, saith, I thirst.

²⁹Now there was set a vessel full of vinegar: and they filled a spunge with vinegar, and put it upon hyssop, and put it to his mouth.

³⁰When Jesus therefore had received the vinegar, he said, it is finished: and he bowed his head, and gave up the ghost.

³¹The Jews therefore, because it was the preparation, that the bodies should not remain upon the cross on the Sabbath day, (for that Sabbath day was an high day,) besought Pilate that their legs might be broken, and that they might be taken away.

³²Then came the soldiers, and brake the legs of the first, and of the other which was crucified with him.

³³But when they came to Jesus, and saw that he was dead already, they brake not his legs:

³⁴But one of the soldiers with a spear pierced his side, and forthwith came there out blood and water.

³⁵And he that saw it bare record and his record is true: and he knoweth that he saith true, that ye might believe.

³⁶For these things were done, that the scripture should be fulfilled, and a bone of him shall not be broken.

³⁷And again another scripture saith, they shall look on him whom they pierced.

³⁸And after this Joseph of Arimathaea, being a disciple of Jesus, but secretly for fear of the Jews, besought Pilate that he might take away the body of Jesus: and Pilate gave him leave. He came therefore, and took the body of Jesus.

³⁹And there came also Nicodemus, which at the first came to Jesus by night, and brought a mixture of myrrh and aloes, about an hundred pound weight.

⁴⁰Then took they the body of Jesus, and wound it in linen clothes with the spices, as the manner of the Jews is to bury.

⁴¹Now in the place where he was crucified there was a garden; and in the garden a new sepulchre, wherein was never man yet laid.

⁴²There laid they Jesus therefore because of the Jews' preparation day; for the sepulchre was nigh at hand.

86- See John 20: 11 thru 18.

¹¹But Mary stood without at the sepulchre weeping: and as she wept, she stooped down, and looked into the sepulchre,

¹²And seeth two angels in white sitting, the one at the head, and the other at the feet, where the body of Jesus had lain.

¹³And they say unto her, Woman, why weepest thou? She saith unto them, because they have taken away my LORD, and I know not where they have laid him.

¹⁴And when she had thus said, she turned herself back, and saw Jesus standing, and knew not that it was Jesus.

¹⁵Jesus saith unto her, Woman, why weepest thou? whom seekest thou? She, supposing him to be the gardener, saith unto him, Sir, if thou have borne him hence, tell me where thou hast laid him, and I will take him away.

¹⁶Jesus saith unto her, Mary. She turned herself, and saith unto him, Rabboni; which is to say, Master.

¹⁷Jesus saith unto her, Touch me not; for I am not yet ascended to my Father: but go to my brethren, and say unto them, I ascend unto my

Father, and your Father; and to my God, and your God.

[18] Mary Magdalene came and told the disciples that she had seen the LORD, and that he had spoken these things unto her.

> This is one reason the very first person Jesus visited after raising from the dead was Mary.
>
> Here is one major clue below which will show that the Disciple who loved him was Mary Magdalene.
>
> First notice, in the KJ Bible, when the God refers to a female, he still uses "He" or "Him" instead of "She" or "Her".
>
> As seen when he was referring to Mirian as being a Prophet.
>
> But yet Mirian was a female, one of the three he was speaking to.

87- See John 21:20 thru 23. Verse 21 man means woman. Also verse 23 he means she.

[20] Then Peter, turning about, seeth the disciple whom Jesus loved following; which also leaned on his breast at supper, and said, Lord, which is he that betrayeth thee?

²¹Peter seeing him saith to Jesus, Lord, and what shall this man do?

²²Jesus saith unto him, **if I will that he tarry till I come**, what is that to thee? Follow thou me.

²³Then went this saying abroad among the brethren, that **that disciple should not die**: yet Jesus said not unto him, **He** shall not die; but, If I will that he tarry till I come, what is that to thee?

88- See Genesis 5:24 contradiction

²⁴And **Enoch walked with God: and he was not; for God took him**.

²⁵And **Methuselah lived an hundred eighty and seven years, and begat Lamech**.

> Don't assume that Enoch went to heaven because a later verse says only Jesus has been the one to be taken up to heaven.

89- See 2 King 2:11 contradiction

¹¹And it came to pass, as they still went on, and talked, that, behold, there appeared a chariot of fire, and horses of fire, and parted them both asunder; and **Elijah went up by a whirlwind into heaven**.

Don't assume that Elijah went to heaven because a later verse says only Jesus has been the one to be taken up to heaven.

90- See 2 Chronicle 9:12 thru 14

¹²And **king Solomon gave to the queen of Sheba all her desire, whatsoever she asked,** beside that which she had brought unto the king. So she turned, and went away to her own land, she and her servants.

¹³Now the weight of gold that came to Solomon in one year was six hundred and threescore and six talents of gold;

¹⁴Beside that which chapmen and merchants brought. **And all the kings of Arabia and governors of the country brought gold and silver to Solomon.**

Verse 13 is 25 tons of Gold which Solomon received.

91- See 1 Corinthians 7:8 Contradiction

⁸I say therefore to the unmarried and widows, **it is good for them if they abide even as I.**

⁹But if they cannot contain, let them marry: for it is better to marry than to burn.

When Paul was in Prison, he wrote letters saying he promoted no marriages; He wanted all to stay single as he was.

92- See 1 John 2:27 Contradiction

²⁷But the anointing which ye have received of him abideth in you, **and ye need not that any man teach you**: but as the same anointing **teacheth you of all things, and is truth, and is no lie,** and even as it hath taught you, ye shall abide in him.

Here he is saying No Teachers are needed. How stupid, God did not leave a handbook for Humans. Back in Biblical times, it might have been so as other people did not want to study deeply as they do now. So many of supposed to be words from God are merely man's words saying what he thinks God would say. How misleading! Many Preachers and men of the cloth do more severe damage by misleading others. They use their own biases to say what God would say and they are wrong. Here below is an example.

93- See Matthew 10:34

³⁴Think not that I am come to send peace on earth: I came not to send peace, but a sword.

The above verse is a really big surprise. I've heard many hundreds of Preachers say that he did bring peace. Also many xmas cards also proclaim **PEACE**. The way it's written, it says he will bring **HAVOC** and hatred.

94- See Numbers 7:5 thru 9.

⁵Take it of them, that they may be to do the service of the tabernacle of the congregation; and thou shalt give them unto the Levites, **to every man according to his service.**

⁶And Moses took the **wagons and the oxen, and gave them unto the Levites.**

⁷**Two wagons and four oxen he gave unto the sons of Gershon, according to their service:**

⁸And **four wagons and eight oxen he gave unto the sons of Merari,** according unto their service, under the hand of Ithamar the son of Aaron the priest.

⁹But unto **the sons of Kohath he gave none**: because the service of the sanctuary belonging unto them was that **they should bear upon their shoulders.**

Kohath had no wagons, no oxen, they had to carry everything on their shoulders.

95- See Judges 1:19 Contradiction

[19] And the LORD was with Judah; and he drave out the inhabitants of the mountain; but **could not drive out the inhabitants of the valley, because they had chariots of iron.**

This kind of statement helps to prove that there was no real, true God helping this expedition. Any kind of chariots would not have been any problem at all at any time for a real, true, loving God. Moses' reason the chariots posed a problem was the running on foot Israel slave army could not keep up nor catch the speeding chariots. Besides, the chariot drivers were marksmen at throwing spears which caused the Israel army to leave the chariots alone. There were many others whom the Israel army couldn't get rid of either. The just co-existed together with them even to this day.

96- See Deuteronomy 20:11 thru 20. Contradiction

[11] And it shall be, if it make thee answer of peace, and open unto thee, then it shall be, **that all the people that is found therein shall be tributaries unto thee, and they shall serve thee.**

[12] And if it will make no peace with thee, but **will make war against thee, then thou shalt besiege it:**

¹³ And **when the LORD thy God hath delivered it into thine hands, thou shalt smite every male thereof with the edge of the sword:**

¹⁴ **But the women, and the little ones, and the cattle, and all that is in the city, even all the spoil thereof, shalt thou take unto thyself; and thou shalt eat the spoil of thine enemies, which the LORD thy God hath given thee.**

¹⁵ **Thus shalt thou do unto all the cities which are very far off from thee**, which are not of the cities of these nations.

¹⁶ But of the cities of these people, which the LORD thy God doth give thee for an inheritance, **thou shalt save alive nothing that breatheth:**

¹⁷ But **thou shalt utterly destroy them; namely, the Hittites, and the Amorites, the Canaanites, and the Perizzites, the Hivites, and the Jebusites;** as the LORD thy God hath commanded thee:

¹⁸ That they teach you not to do after all their abominations, which they have done unto their gods; so should ye sin against the LORD your God.

¹⁹ When thou shalt besiege a city a long time, in making war against it to take it, **thou shalt not destroy the trees thereof by forcing an axe against them: for thou mayest eat of them, and thou shalt not cut them down (for the tree of the field is man's life) to employ them in the siege:**

²⁰Only the trees which thou knowest that they be not trees for meat, thou shalt destroy and cut them down; and thou shalt build bulwarks against the city that maketh war with thee, until it be subdued.

Verse 14 says the army is allowed to take the women and children and all the cattle and everything in the city can be taken as your reward.

97- See Exodus 32:27 thru 28. Contradiction

²⁷And he said unto them, Thus saith the LORD God of Israel, **Put every man his sword by his side, and go in and out from gate to gate throughout the camp, and slay every man his brother, and every man his companion, and every man his neighbour.**

²⁸And the children of Levi did according to the word of Moses: and there fell of the people that day about three thousand men.

> Above, Moses had the Levi Police to put on their swords and kill their own relatives in their own camp. They practiced with their swords and killed about 3,000 that day.
>
> The more I read, the more I am convinced that these are not actual a God's words. It's a Mad-man wanting power and he is a slave driver in many, many, of these verses. He dis-

plays our God as a mean, not loving, no value for human life God.

It took them 40 years to make it across the desert from Egypt to the Canaan land. But not far really! Especially with a real, true, loving God's help.

The distance straight across only going East from Egypt to that same Canaan land would have take only a few weeks to travel. They could have made it in only one season. Just think, two or three months verus over 40 years. Hogwash!

Remember the area down in Midian where he found a wife, well he wanted to take his army back that same way to impress his Father-In-Law of what he had accomplished. Also he took the whole, over a million people with him to help convince his Father-In-Law to go along with them to the new promised land. But Jethro said no, He had more daughters to go home to see and be with.

Don't forget that Moses planned that his army needed lots of training time periods to go to war. He had to settle in the desert to accomplish much long training. He knew that he could not go straight east direct to Canaan. He knew that his army needed time to get violent, ruff, rude and able to kill all the previous land owners to get the Promised Land.

Besides, he wanted to spend one whole year building a huge big tent to house his pretended God's new home.

His secret scrolls were also buried on God's mountain that he had to go back for. The scrolls he made earlier in his life that I have explained within this book. They were his extremely valuable papers he needed to perform his Master Slave driver duties later thru out all his life. In those scrolls were his notes for new laws of how people should act and behave also. He had an extensive start on all the modified rules gathered in his own home's Pharaoh's Palace court.

I have told all about these valuable scrolls earlier in my book.

98- See Exodus 30:12 thru 21.

^{12}When thou takest the sum of the children of Israel after their number, then shall **they give every man a ransom for his soul unto the LORD,** when thou numberest them; that there be no plague among them, when thou numberest them.

^{13}This they shall give, every one that passeth among them that are numbered, **half a shekel after the** shekel of the sanctuary: (a shekel is twenty gerahs:) an half shekel shall be the offering of the LORD.

[14]Every one that passeth among them that are numbered, **from twenty years old and above, shall give an offering unto the LORD.**

[15]The rich shall not give more, and the poor shall not give less than half a shekel, when they give an offering unto the LORD, **to make an atonement for your souls.**

[16]And thou shalt take the atonement money of the children of Israel, and shalt appoint it for the service of the tabernacle of the congregation; that it may be a memorial unto the children of Israel before the LORD, **to make an atonement for your souls.**

[17]And the LORD spake unto Moses, saying,

[18]Thou shalt also make a laver of brass, and his foot also of brass, to wash withal: and thou shalt put it between the tabernacle of the congregation and the altar, **and thou shalt put water therein.**

[19]**For Aaron and his sons shall wash their hands and their feet thereat:**

[20]When they go into the tabernacle of the congregation, **they shall wash with water, that they die not;** or when they come near to the altar to minister, to burn offering made by fire unto the LORD:

²¹So they shall wash their hands and their feet, that they die not: and it shall be a statute for ever to them, even to him and to his seed throughout their generations.

The above is orders that each man counted is paid for his soul and no plague will bother him.

99- See Joshua 5:4 thru 15. Contradiction

⁴And this is the cause why Joshua did circumcise: All the people that came out of Egypt, that were males, even **all the men of war, died in the wilderness by the way, after they came out of Egypt.**

⁵Now all the people that came out were circumcised: **but all the people that were born in the wilderness by the way as they came forth out of Egypt, them they had not circumcised.**

⁶**For the children of Israel walked forty years in the wilderness, till all the people that were men of war, which came out of Egypt, were consumed, because they obeyed not the voice of the LORD: unto whom the LORD sware that he would not shew them the land,** which the LORD sware unto their fathers that he would give us, a land that floweth with milk and honey.

⁷And their children, whom he raised up in their stead, them Joshua circumcised: for they were un-

circumcised, because they had not circumcised them by the way.

⁸And it came to pass, when they had done circumcising all the people, that they abode in their places in the camp, till they were whole.

⁹And the LORD said unto Joshua, This day have I rolled away the reproach of Egypt from off you. Wherefore **the name of the place is called Gilgal unto this day.**

¹⁰And the children of Israel encamped in Gilgal, and kept the passover on the fourteenth day of the month at even **in the plains of Jericho.**

¹¹And they did eat of the old corn of the land on the morrow after the passover, unleavened cakes, and parched corn in the selfsame day.

¹²And **the manna ceased on the morrow after they had eaten of the old corn of the land; neither had the children of Israel manna any more; but they did eat of the fruit of the land of Canaan that year.**

¹³And it came to pass, when Joshua was by Jericho, that he lifted up his eyes and looked, and, behold, **there stood a man over against him with his sword drawn in his hand: and Joshua went unto him,** and said unto him, Art thou for us, or for our adversaries?

¹⁴And he said, Nay; but as captain of the host of the LORD am I now come. And Joshua fell on his face to the earth, and did worship, and said unto him, What saith my Lord unto his servant?

¹⁵And the captain of the LORD's host said unto Joshua, Loose thy shoe from off thy foot; for the place whereon thou standest is holy. And Joshua did so.

> **Verse 13 says a man with a sword was standing over Joshua. How stupid of Joshua to just bow down not knowing if that man was an enemy or not, ready to kill Joshua. You don't just ask a man while war is going on "Are thou for us"? Wouldn't he lie and kill you anyway. I know that the Bible writer wanted to make the reader believe the Lord; God was once again on the Israel's army side. Hogwash.**

100- See John 3:16 Contradiction with below verse.

¹⁶For God so loved the world, that **he gave his only begotten Son**, that whosoever believeth in him should not perish, but have everlasting life

101- See Genesis 6: 4 Contradiction with above verse.

⁴There were giants in the earth in those days; and also after that, **when the sons of God came in unto**

the daughters of men, and they bare children to them, the same became mighty men which were of old, men of renown.

Many more sons of God. That is why he gave a tree in Eden which would give eternal life to his chosen.

102- See Exodus 9:1 thru 4 Contradiction.

¹Then the LORD said unto Moses, Go in unto Pharaoh, and tell him, Thus saith the LORD God of the Hebrews, Let my people go, that they may serve me.

²For if thou refuse to let them go, and wilt hold them still,

³Behold, **the hand of the LORD is upon thy cattle which is in the field, upon the horses, upon the asses, upon the camels, upon the oxen, and upon the sheep: there shall be a very grievous murrain.**

⁴And **the LORD shall sever between the cattle of Israel and the cattle of Egypt: and there shall nothing die of all that is the children's of Israel.**

> Moses and his brother, did ten different tricks or plagues for the Pharaoh. The number five was to kill all the cows, horses of the Egyptains but it did not happen and is a Contradiction as further after they left Egypt,

over 600 horses was used to pull the fine chariots. Meaning that they did not die earlier. It said that all Egypt's Livestock died when the Plague struck,

103- See Matthew 15:10 thru 11 Contradiction.

¹⁰And he called the multitude, and **said unto them, Hear, and understand:**

¹¹**Not that which goeth into the mouth defileth a man;** but that which cometh out of the mouth, this defileth a man.

¹²Then came his disciples, and said unto him, **Knowest thou that the Pharisees were offended, after they heard this saying?**

Back in the Biblical times, No knowledge was know about drinking bad water, eating spoils or the such. **Since modern times, we are told wash your hands often or some germ might enter your mouth and cause terrible sickness or even death.**

104- See Numbers 16:20 thru 23. Contradiction

²⁰And the LORD spake unto Moses and unto Aaron, saying,

²¹**Separate yourselves from among this congregation, that I may consume them in a moment.**

²²And they fell upon their faces, and said, O God, the God of the spirits of all flesh, shall one man sin, and wilt thou be wroth with all the congregation?

²³And the LORD spake unto Moses, saying,

> **In verse 21 above, it was said by the supposed God that he wanted to kill the entire army. He wanted Moses to get away from the slaves so he could kill them all at once.**
>
> **I have many dozens more but because of space and time, I will stop here. Thank you, Professor Roy Yonce.**

Reading and taking notes, suggested plan.

The complete K J Holy Bible consists of 66 books.

39 books make up the Old Testament and 27 books make up the New Testament.

Where to start and which one to study for your best comprehension ability.

Start with the Old Testament first. Read only the first eight books, in sequential order.

Get that much understood as best you can. If you take notes, then by all means if you find out your notes were not laid out in a sequential plan that was good enough with space between so you can add more details on a later reading, then start your note taking again. Discard your old notes and refer to the new ones. Notes are always needed from any subject one tries to study. It's a great way to have better controlled remembering of facts, details, and comprehension.

After understanding the first eight books, with great referenced notes. By the time you have read and understood these 8 books pretty well of the Old Testament, then skip over to start your New Testament comprehension.

Read only the first 5 books in sequential order of the New Testament. With note taking just like you did in the Old Testament.

When you have finished these five books of the New Testament, you only have one more really rough and mean violence filled materials book to read for all your best Old and New Testament comprehension. Read Revelations, it's a bear cat to handle. There are many books in both, The Old and the New Testament which should only be read to children. (Not turned loose to read on their own) or nightmares visit.

Then you only have 21 letters (Correspondence) which were written by Paul and others to read in the New Testament. These are not at all needed at first to have a good comprehension and understanding of the complete K J Bible.

The Letters that make up the New Testament are just polish to add to your information already acquired and it is suggested you get that at the very last.

I pointed out to all of my College students, that they might lose respect from some of their relations and even loved ones because they were not informed nor attempted to learn more of the things which helps the world go round. Things they could offer their own opinions on in life's chosen trail. But how could they even act or be an informed citizen about any subject they refused to look into?

One particular old time, very impressionable person named Leonardo da Vinci proved that the mind never gets tired of learning so one should endeavor to learn all he/she can.

I wish there was a God to help, Poem

Composed, written and printed by:
Professor Roy Yonce

I have lived a very long life, never have I seen an Intervening God,

Many happenings, millions killed, all sorts of calamities, always changing the destined sod.

I'd really like to see a loving Supreme, show his work,

But the King James Bible proves, with man's biases, Moses was a jerk.

Others that reap his tax deductions, try to show his full lovings indeed,

But by reading that Bible, one finds out jealousy, hatred, and anger was his creed.

I have searched the whole complete Bible for enough words to follow,

But a slave driver, none loving, cruelness to others is very hard to swallow.

In the stories, he promised a future acquired land with milk and honey,

They did not know they had to spy, fight, die, break the commandments, Wow! It just wasn't funny.

His set of 10 commandments included "Thou shalt not steal",

But that is exactly what each had to do, in order to ever, the land to feel.

His set of 10 commandments also said "Thou shalt not kill",

But each soldier of Israel's army realized they had to do it and for real.

They murdered millions and more, wives, livestock, buried their towns,

They numbered over 600,000 taking what the thieves wanted absolutely, it sounds.

Moses will tell the story that God did help, but who needs a God, Him,

When over 600,000 with swords go marching in, No one is out on a limb.

In the stories, Moses tells how God ask for all 600,000 to go along,

That's ridiculous with that many swords, going home, all would have a song.

The King James Bible has many major contradictions in print,

Read Professor Roy Yonce's book. He points out a rather lying scoundrel as he was sent.

You will read how God is supposed to deliver a promised land,

But only after taking over 1 million slaves, 40 years through the hot sandy desert walking by each man.

God in these Bible stories made the slaves manufacture a meeting tent,

Hundreds of walkers with lots of weight on their shoulders, they were sent.

In the stories, Moses was raised in the Kings Palace, hiding his fate,

Because the King had issued an order, "Throw all male Hebrew children in the river as alligator bait".

When Moses was grown, he wandered out of the King's Palace, a murderer he became,

Then he had to leave his loving foster mother, go into the desert, a fugitive, his aim.

Read the marvelous story yourself, but remember to keep to yourself, your wit,

You will find in the fabricated tales, an extremely jealous, none loving God always telling his slaves, Shut your mouths and Lets git!

All Rights Reserved
Copyright © 2010 by Professor Roy Yonce
No part of this book may be reproduced or transmitted in any form or by any means, electronic or mechanical, including photocopying, recording, or by any information storage and retrieval system without permission in writing from the author.